W9-BDH-311

DISCARD

The Edges
of the
Civilized World

Also by Alison Hawthorne Deming

Nonfiction

Temporary Homelands
Girls in the Jungle

Poetry

Science and Other Poems
The Monarchs
Poetry of the American West (editor)

The Edges
of the
Civilized World

a journey in
nature and culture

Alison Hawthorne Deming

Picador USA   New York

Picador® is a U.S. registered trademark and is used by St. Martin's Press
under license from Pan Books Limited.

Grateful acknowledgment goes to the following publications in which this
work first appeared: *Creative Nonfiction, The Georgia Review, Islands: An
International Magazine, Poetry Flash, Orion: People and Nature,* and *Sonora
review.* "Poetry and Science: A View from the Divide" won the Bayer Award
in science writing from *Creative Nonfiction.*

"I, Nezahualcoyotl" reprinted with permission from *Fifteen Poets of the
Aztec Word* by Miguel Leon-Portilla, University of Oklahoma Press.
Copyright © 1992 by Miguel Leon-Portilla. Lines from "Why Gambling
Is Spiritual" by Jim Cohn from *Grasslands* by Jim Cohn. Published in 1994
by Writers & Books Publications, Rochester, New York. Reprinted
with permission.

Library of Congress Cataloging-in-Publication Data

Deming, Alison Hawthorne.
    The edges of the civilized world / Alison Deming.
        p.   cm.
    ISBN 0-312-19543-5
    1. Nature.   2. Culture.   I. Title.
QH81.D44   1998
508—DC21   98-18714
                                                    CIP

DESIGN BY JAMES SINCLAIR

First Picador USA Edition: November 1998

10 9 8 7 6 5 4 3 2 1

I accept with all my heart and with gratitude what nature has done for me, and I am pleased with myself and proud of myself that I do.

—Michel de Montaigne

As a consequence of this complex history of our species, most beings long to recapture now and then each of the various experiences of their evolutionary past: that of the hunter-gatherer, of the farmer and pastoralist, and of the urban dweller. The wooing of Earth thus implies much more than converting the wilderness into humanized environments. It means also preserving environments in which to experience mysteries transcending daily life and from which to recapture, in a Proustian kind of remembrance, the awareness of the cosmic forces that have shaped mankind.

—René Dubos

It is at the periphery that I can come to understand the central issues of living.

—Hugh Brody

contents

Acknowledgments

I am indebted to many friends and colleagues who helped nourish this book through gifts of conversation, shared meals and travels, and their own insightful art. My thanks for the generosity of spirit and mind that came from W. S. Di Piero, Gary Paul Nabhan, Joanne Mulcahy and Bob Hazen, Joan Marshall, David and Phyllis Burks, Richard Nelson, Pattiann Rogers, John Daniel, Richard Shelton, David Abram, Karl Kim, Alden Borders, Scott Slovic, Tom Christensen, Tomi Knaefler, George Huey, Paul Spitzer, and Carolyn Servid. Lucinda Bliss has been a keen reader of early drafts, and I thank her for taking time from her painting to do so. Joan Tapper at *Islands* sent me on assignment to the Sea of Cortés, the quiet adventure that launched this project. Chip Blake at *Orion* offered invaluable editorial focus on a chapter that appeared first in that magazine. The University of Arizona has provided me a comfortable professional home, as well as time off for good behavior so that I could complete this work. An opportunity to teach for a semester at the University of Hawai'i moved my imagination far enough West that I could begin to see the East. I thank both institutions, as well as the many talented students whose energy continues to prompt mine.

Fellowships from the National Endowment for the Arts and the Arizona Commission on the Arts gave me time for travel, research and writing, without which I could not have completed this book.

For their continued faith in my work, and the deadline that urged me productively on, my heartfelt thanks go to Jennie McDonald and George Witte.

The Edges
of the
Civilized World

Prologue: Pacific City

Early morning—the opening edge of the day. I walk out over frost-rimed sand, under a clear winter sky, cross a deer trail in the swale of the dunes, then an etching of bird tracks that leads to the glistening margin where the Pacific slips onto the land and recedes. A flock of sanderlings works the intertidal zone, racing on little stilted legs from the incoming wave, then turning around to hastily feed on the slick of small organisms the wave leaves behind, chasing the water back out to sea until its energy subsides and the new wave sends the birds racing back shoreward. They seem never to mistime the turning point and become engulfed by the rushing water. They seem to have an intuitive sense about this, since they train their eyes on the wet ground where they forage and not on the sea. They are utterly present in their task and, without any evidence of anticipation, they know how to do the right thing.

At this hour there are no people on the beach, no pickup trucks or Jeeps, no jet-skiers or surfers. There is the foot track of one early walker. And my own. There is a strip of sand three miles long that borders the sea, running from the mouth of the Nestucca River at one end to the banded escarpment of Cape Kiwanda on the other. Offshore stands a stout sea stack several hundred feet tall—Haystack Rock—that offers a stabilizing counterpoint to the perpetual motion of the swells and eddies surrounding it. A slender arch on the stone's northern edge looks like the eye of a needle. The rock is one of the distinguishing features of the town. I'm not sure why its form is so pleasing, but when one approaches Pacific City and first sees that natural monument presiding over the modest strand of beach houses, the placid river, and the boiling surf, one feels there is something in the place to contemplate.

I have come to this quiet spot on the northern Oregon coast to feed on a question, or constellation of questions, that has troubled me. What is civilization? Where and how is it being formed? On what assumptions is it founded? What should we hope for the future of humanity and our world? To what extent can our ideas, hopes and will shape the future? What has civilization blurred and rejected that we might clarify and call back into our shepherding intelligence? What lessons did our ancestors learn that we should not forget? And what of their practices would we be better off in leaving behind? It is the late twentieth century, and one can do nothing without doubts and questions. We see everything from multiple perspectives: most of civilization's gains have been earned at the expense of others, and for all of its marvelous advances civilization has led the natural world to the edge of collapse. We can count, like numbers on a doomsday clock, the species being driven out of existence. We can measure the hole we have made in the sky and the dirty pall that threatens to smother the Earth. We can predict the outcome of continuing to consume the world, but we cannot seem to stop ourselves from consuming it. The result seems to be that one either revels in consumption and forgets the future, or one retreats into solipsistic rage, lament and self-hatred. "If humanity's the enemy," writes poet Chase Twichell, "the enemy is me."

Knowing that civilization has been the royal standard under

which conquest, genocide and enslavement have been committed throughout history, how can one justly consider civilization's spiritual aspect: the good progress of humanity as we struggle to transcend the qualities in ourselves that rob us of faith in our own nature and rob others of their future? What antidote can be found to counteract the poison of anticipating an apocalyptic future in which human power destroys not only its own best inventions, but the very conditions under which life is given? Can we restore faith in civilization as an expression of radical hope in the best of the collective human enterprise on Earth—those acts and accomplishments that honor beauty, wisdom, understanding, inventiveness, love and moral connection with others?

Perhaps such questions are not the province of art, which thrives on being present in the moment, on attending to what's local, peculiar, off-kilter and half-seen. Or perhaps such questions are the only province of art—the attempt to understand, as John Haines once put it, the terms of one's existence. Art is a materialization of the inner life, so when a question persists, no matter its unwieldy or hazy nature, one knows one is stuck with it—it is the needle though which one must pass the thread.

I began to think about these questions while traveling among the uninhabited islands in the Sea of Cortés, an area of wild and fragile refuge from the pressures of consumerist development. The virtue of travel to such places is that one can experience a renewal of the sense of belonging in and to the natural world. But such renewal has become harder and harder to find as the earth's living fabric has become more tattered. The edges of civilization, for millennia, have been defined by migrations, expeditions and voyages of discovery that opened new territory and new cultural and natural relationships. Now the edges of civilization are defined by the incremental disappearance of the natural world.

After spending a happy week sailing from one pristine anchorage to the next, hiking into remote expanses of endemic cacti and blooming wildflowers too rare to be found in the best field guide, I returned to the port of La Paz, capital of Baja California Sur, to read newspaper headlines reporting a legislative clearing of the way for a resort and casino proposed for one of the most spectacular islands of the reserve, Isla del Espíritu Santo, a jewel of geologic and botanic wonders. I felt again how fragile all wildness has become. I had been traveling not in the wilderness, it seemed, but along the edges of the civilized world—a fault line where pressure constantly builds, where the impingement of economic necessity abrades against nature.

I have felt this abrasion most keenly not in cities, but in remoter places—places as disparate as southern Mexico, Atlantic Canada, the Rocky Mountain West, Hawai'i, and the Pacific Northwest. In each of these places natural-resource-based ways of life have declined, and local people have looked to tourism development as a new way to extract a livelihood out of their place. When I first arrived in Pacific City (really only a small coastal town), I told a friendly innkeeper that I was writing about places undergoing such a change. "Oh, that's Pacific City," she encouraged, explaining how declines in logging, fishing and farming had led townspeople to try to sell the beauty of the place in the form of vacation homes and weekend getaways.

It is easy for people to anticipate the economic benefits of tourism development, but hard for them to factor in the costs to local nature and culture. Certainly it is a gain if ancient trees are worth more standing in the forest than cut for the pulpmill. But when a place becomes a playground, long-standing equations written between the land and people are rewritten, and the rich-

ness of a local lifeway based on intimate working knowledge of
the land is heavily taxed. Everywhere I went and explained my
project, people said, "Oh, that's Colorado," or "Oh, that's
Hawai'i," and I began to realize that such change was happening
nearly everywhere during this age when humanity sprawls across
the world, ever eager for new experience and opportunity, ever
ready to turn a new limitation into some kind of growth. Nature
makes its presence felt, wrote Hannah Arendt, "in the man-made
world through the constant threat of overgrowing and decaying
it." And humanity makes its presence felt in nature with such a
threat.

The beach at Pacific City reinvents itself every day. One afternoon after a blustering storm that slammed horizontal rain
against the south wall of my cabin, I walked out to find that the
sand had been sculpted into tiny mesas—a bit of bark or seaweed, pebble or shell, teetering on a pedestal of sand, the wind
having swept the surrounding grains away, but the weight of the
tiny objects keeping the sand sculptures in place. They appeared
in clusters, little cities designed by chance. There were great fins
of sand fanning back from drift logs that had broken the sweeping force of the wind. By the time I walked from one end of the
beach to the other, the tide had come in and wiped out all the
newly invented forms.

   Other days it is black sand that makes its mark on the beach.
I think I am looking at water-shaped ripples in the sand, but
when I get close, I find an elegant pattern drawn by the wind in
black and tan grains. After a flood that closed many coastal
roads, rivers breaching banks and berms and stranding herds of
dairy cows so that they could not be milked for days, the beach
was heaped with torn trees, cracked twigs, bulbed bullwhips of

uprooted kelp, litter of brown spruce and fir needles, and dead pelagic birds. The next day those heaps had disappeared. I wondered where so much debris might go in a single day, until I stepped onto a thin crust of newly blown sand that gave way, drawing me down to the knee in that storm's buried trash.

On my walks I often see great flocks of geese or ducks flying from the north in a lazy V toward the river. They look like black musical notes written on the sky. At low tide I often find jellyfish stranded on the wet ground—globs of clear gelatinous stuff, some with a scalloped edge, some with a starlike dome, the collapsed purple organs and pale white filigree of tentacles so delicate as to be barely visible. Waves pummel the shore, four or five cresting at once. The moment each wave climbs into its perfect curl is the moment it tumbles apart—so exquisite and temporary, this ordered falling of energy into and out of a form. In these moments the world feels complete and perfect.

But the human imagination cannot rest long in timeless reverie. A beautiful place is an invitation for people to inhabit it. The beach I walk, while being wild and open on its ocean side, is lined with beach houses on the landward side: Pacific City— elevation seven feet, population one thousand. A large resort hotel and microbrewery are slated for construction at one end of the beach, and a luxury home is going up on the pristine headland at the other end. Developments of several hundred houses are sprouting, and properties are selling overnight for cash. Those private gains will be a loss in terms of the commonwealth of unrestricted land. I try not to resent this, knowing that the one sure thing about the future is that people will be more numerous. We will have to learn to live more closely with others, so we had all better learn to stop hating our numerousness.

Certainly those who feel these changes most keenly as a loss are the locals who have lived here all their lives. "When we were kids, they wouldn't even let us walk on those dunes," said the woman who cut my hair, alarmed to see a development going up on fragile sand. "I'm really not in favor of progress," said another, complaining about the new checkout aisles and scanners at Lew's Market. "I prefer for things to stay funky."

Pacific City is a town at the crux of a change. Above the lowland cluster of houses and shops, the one four-way red blinker beating like a miniature heart at the center of town, rise steep hills, a few wooded, most ravaged by clear-cutting down to the bare, scabbed ground. The Nestucca River bends through town—indeed, gives the town its weaving linear shape, the settlement of houses tracing the river's course. Chinook and coho salmon still run here; it is one of the best wild rivers in Oregon and one of the last not ruined for salmon by dams. Sport fishermen meet the swimmers as they head inland from the Pacific to spawn. Anglers follow the migration upstream until the fish have exhausted themselves in the urgencies of breeding and die. The sight of this seasonal rite was one of the things that charmed me about the town when I arrived in October. I watched a crowd of fishermen lining the river where it passes under the town bridge. They stood a few feet apart, each casting into the river's gentle churn, and I, who can barely cast a line without tangling it in my own gear, marveled at the graceful order of fourteen fishing lines dancing out to the depths and back, over and under one another, with never a confounding intersection.

Back at the motel I watched an old man in yellow rubber overalls cleaning a forty-pound hen salmon on the picnic table—a tall, cragged timber of a man wearing wraparound shades, a webbed baseball cap and blood. He cut the carcass in cubes to smoke and can, the flesh so shiny orange it spoke of life even dead. The man walked with pain, a crick in his leg, and his movements slowed by age. Yet I felt the ritual pleasure he took in the task, and I assumed the practice was as habitual for him as the salmon's climb upriver from the sea.

But fishing is a sport here, not an industry. And while the timber harvest for the state last year totaled 4,167 million board feet, according to the Oregon Department of Forestry, that number is by far the lowest in the past twenty-five years. What remains of the ancient forests in the Northwest is not sufficient to predict anything but a steady decline in logging as a way to make a living. Dairy farms appear to thrive along the county's green fertile riverbeds, but it seems safe to speculate that the family farm here, as elsewhere on the continent, requires more muscle labor and produces more modest monetary rewards than most young people, whose desires like everyone else's are being educated by television and Hollywood, will find appealing for much longer—particularly as they taste the temptation created by the rising real estate values that accompany tourist development. It seems odd to me that land becomes more valuable when it comes to mean *less* to people in terms of the meaning that can come from working the land.

I don't wish to romanticize the past by suggesting that the way people used to inhabit the land was necessarily better than what's to come. Certainly there are virtues to the changes, not the least of which is that tourists who come to Pacific City primarily to enjoy the beauty of the place will tread more lightly on the land than those whose livelihood is earned with a chain saw and skidder. And certainly there is a virtue to building the kind of home that makes a beautiful statement about people's relationship with the land and the sea. But there is a sadness in seeing a dozen cozy fishermen's cabins strung along a bend in the river fall to mossy ruin, while big glassy monolithic homes and gated communities go in down the road. And there is a chilling sense that the working people of this town, those who live in the trailer park or the run-down houses, the places with a bleach-bottle weather vane or a black pickup truck labeled "Land Shark" may soon be sent for the poor hills inland, and the town, though it will look a lot more perfect, will lose a little of its soul.

In the cold winter morning I walk past Haystack Rock and climb the steep dune to the top of Cape Kiwanda. There is a place here I call the Cauldron, though no sign or trail marker identifies it or tells the history of its meanings to local residents. Only a tattered, rusty chain-link fence that makes the place look like a closed amusement park. From the first time I happened upon it, I felt it to be a sacred place, because it sparked a quality of attention quite out of the ordinary, tapping into the quiet place in *me* that remains in harmony with the world, no matter what arguments with it I wage. The sea has cut a narrow bending slot cove in the coastal sandstone, an invagination that the seawater enters full of all its masculine strength. But, like any phenomenon worth repeated examination, it is more complex than one metaphor can convey. Its complexity is what makes it fascinating.

The polished sandstone of the cape is ribboned with layers of mineral stain, its surface worn so smooth it looks like clay freshly molded, revealing the rock's once liquid nature. Waves break where the cove narrows, then fracture into chunks of wave that slam into the channel, scattering in a wildly orchestrated array of motions—climbing a gigantic fin of rock and sweeping down to a ledge at its base, sluicing up a precipice to backwash slowly over a lip of softened stone, spurling into clouds of froth that melt back to nothing, flowing up through a large keyhole to fan out on a scallop-shaped amphitheater of stone, pounding into a cave, backsplashing through a crevasse to form a long slender spume, and spouting out of a breathing hole high on the cliff. There is a green algal stain to the horizontal surfaces, a dark mineral leaching to the vertical ones. When the tide is right, a small flock of black turnstones feed in the thin wash of the scallop-shaped ledge, pacing and repeating their rattling song.

The sounds at the Cauldron are as rich and complex as the sights—the slam of surf against rock, the roar of falling water, the slosh, slap and gush of it finding its way, the splatter and trickle, the boom in the cave where inrushing water turns to thunder, and the blowhole's breathy gush as muscular as that of a whale. The multiplicity of movement and sound is complex, and yet it feels ordered—so much chaos, and yet it speaks in a voice that is simple and clear, retelling what must be the most enduring story on earth: as things are worn apart, new things are given form. This lesson, transposed from the mineral to the spiritual realm, suggests that each loss defines a new possibility, that despair over the fate of the world may define the edges of hope.

I have walked to the Cauldron many times—alone or with a friend, with notebook or sketchpad or camera. Each time I have walked away feeling that I have apprenticed myself to wisdom. How a place can have wisdom I do not know. How it can communicate that wisdom I also do not know. But I know that my imagination, my ability to dream about the world's possibilities, is as much a product of place as are those banded sandstone cliffs, minutely redefined by erosion every day.

And so I have carried my questions to a few distinctive places, giving a voice to geographic and mental habitats located on the borders of change.

chapter 1

The Value of Experience

There is no desire more natural than the desire for knowledge.
We try all the ways that can lead us to it. When reason fails
us, we use experience.

—Michel de Montaigne

Whenever I was sick as a child, I had a fever dream in which a tree that looked as lobed and meaty as a brain would grow uncontrollably, consuming everything in sight. I was a part of the time-lapse mushrooming and yet I could stand apart and witness it. One time I woke from this experience in a night terror, feeling that I had nearly lost myself to its burgeoning. I sat up straight and turned on the light. The hands of my alarm clock were racing like a movie calendar in which ten years pass in ten seconds' time. At this rate, I thought, my life won't last very long. And I willed myself to slow down the clock. I did not question whether it was possible for me to do this. It was necessary and, in that moment of terrified awareness, the ability came as a gift. And that is how I learned about the power of the human imagination, not in school, not in museums, not in books, not in therapy. Later, of course, all of those instruments of learning proved valuable to me. But first came a paradoxical experience of the power of the mind to create and destroy and re-create its own reality.

Montaigne was so fascinated by his own experience he vowed "to study it, savor it, and ruminate it" rather than let it fly by like sleep without being conscious of it. "To the end that sleep itself should not escape me thus stupidly," he wrote, "at one time I saw fit to have mine disturbed, so that I might gain a glimpse of it." And why not begin one's study of the world with inspecting the basic machinery of one's intelligence: we learn by remembering and telling others what has happened to us, by putting our stories together until a pattern forms and we begin together to understand something we could not understand alone. Writing is like that. One hashes over one's experience looking for patterns and order, feeling an intuition of form, like a scratchy throat before getting the flu. And one may regret experiencing this symptom, because writing a book—wanting to write a book—can feel a lot like having an illness that one cannot shake. But if one gets really sick and recovers, there may be a something to show for it that recounts individual experience in a way that has collective meaning.

The value of experience does not pertain only to one's self; it is by Darwin's definition what distinguishes intelligence from instinct. Intelligence may exist as a continuum spanning all living creatures, but the ability to learn from experience and rapidly adapt based on learning is what separates the human beings from the bugs. The female digger wasp, for example, will maintain several burrows for her maturing offspring. Each morning, she will inspect the burrows to determine which contain eggs requiring no food, which contain larvae needing two or three caterpillars to eat, and which contain pupated offspring to be sealed in for metamorphosis. On the basis of her inspection, the wasp knows how much prey to capture and where to deliver the food. If the occupants of the burrows are switched after her morning inspection, she will spend the day delivering caterpillars to a burrow containing eggs; she will examine an egg many times without realizing it needs no food; and she will seal off young larvae to starve. Her instinctual behavior is based on the findings of her morning inspection, and it offers a very limited opportunity for learning from experience.

Human beings have unlimited opportunities for learning, remembering, and passing on the lessons experience teaches us, finding ever more efficient means to communicate them to one another, and we are all the smarter for one another's learning. Where we find a limit in our biological capacities, we invent a technology to extend our reach. When our habitat becomes depleted, we move to another or, increasingly, try to restore what we have lost. We seem to be infinitely plastic in shaping ourselves to new realities, and learning voraciously in order to do so. What is puzzling about the state of human beings in our consumerist heyday is that we do not place much value on learning from experience. We value things, and go about acquiring them as if we were novice hunter-gatherers needing to forage constantly in order to survive. We measure progress in economic terms, not in natural or cultural ones. Once linked to nature as the commonwealth of all living beings, we have traded that alliance for one with the human economy. But if we reported each year's progress not in terms of fiscal loss and gain but in terms of the earth's biological and cultural loss and gain, we would have a more accurate assessment of human success.

For days and weeks I work over volumes of notes taken on two trips to Mexico, transcribing them from handwritten notebook to computer disk, being careful to remain accurate to the facts: an old man sweeping with a twig broom, a woman carrying an enormous basket of gardenias on her head, a truckload of *federales* buying Cokes in a seri village, a fig tree in a remote island arroyo carved with the words "I love you," the carcass of a freshly slaughtered calf lashed with rope into a wheelbarrow, the throaty word and grazing of fingertips—not a handshake but a gesture local and ancient—as Zapotec women greet each other on a bus. Each entry records a moment at which I felt exquisitely alive in apprehending something new and particular, something American yet utterly foreign, that made me see a border in my mind I had never crossed.

I amass all the entries, review them in the context of one another, highlighting those that still provide a bolus of energy. Yet I find no shape, no order, no pattern to lend meaning to my hoard. It looks more like life than art, a flood of experience that races through time without slowing down to form a calm, reflective pool. If I were an anthropologist, linguist, historian or botanist, I would bring an articulated research question on my travels. I would gather aggregate data to support my hypothesis or failing that frame a new research question based on inconclusive findings. I would propose a theory or venture an argument or make something useful—an interpretation, a dictionary, a policy statement or a pharmaceutical formula. But I am a poet: a maker of poems, which are useful only in the way that dreams are, as vessels for particular experience.

And I confess personal qualities associated with the figurative sense of the word: the poet gives herself to being moved imaginatively and emotionally, she savors the intensities of consciousness, she is a novelty seeker in the inner domain as an adventurer is in the outer, she is drawn to the light of beauty and to the darkness that gives beauty its shape. Such qualities made poets so dangerous to Plato that he banned us from his utopian city. I turned from poetry to writing prose not in order to become more journalistic, utilitarian or argumentative, but simply to bring more of my experience of the world onto the page. I brought with me a faith in the value of writing based on personal experience as an instrument through which culture might see itself. To value experience in a thing-loving age necessitates elevating experience to the status of things. One device for doing that is art. That makes the process sound mechanical. In practice it feels organic. First I forage about in the world, then I forage about in my notebooks, and somewhere along the way, if I am lucky, I start to hear some music I can dance to. And then the steps reveal a pattern, and the dancing becomes more confident and sensual. I do it in the dark, circling in the arms of the world, sometimes leading, sometimes following, always in love with the possibility of greater wakefulness and how it might heal the actual wounds of living.

For this, Plato banished us. For what would become of civilization if we were all to dance with ourselves in the dark?

I traveled to Mexico looking for a missing part of myself. I don't mean that I was looking for family roots. I have none there, though my grandmother lived in Mexico City for several years at the turn of the century. As a young woman she had entered an arranged marriage with an older Cuban man whom her parents believed to be of a class to properly care for her. They had emigrated from France to New York City, and such arrangements were the family's tradition, a widely respected marital strategy at the time. Little of my grandmother's story has survived her. I never thought to ask for details while she was alive. Apparently her husband had been what polite society would have called a roué. He had caused his parents so much trouble that they decided to set up the newlyweds far away from whatever history of embarrassments he had written in New York. For my grandmother, the marriage was a happy time. They had lived an aristocratic life in Mexico City. A witty French girl with magnificent clothes (her mother had been a dress designer), she had so charmed the President of Mexico that he gave her a horse. She lived with us when I was a child, and she loved calling me into her room to look through her artifacts: here she was standing proudly beside her mount in front of their city home; here she was dressed as Carmen, a fat cigar raised coquettishly near her lips; and here was the infant who had died at birth dressed in funeral lace. Her husband had died of consumption soon thereafter, and she had returned to New York with the photographs, some castanets, and a magnificent embroidered Spanish shawl that she would unfold from its tissue-paper storage. Perhaps my attraction to Mexico began when those few images from my grandmother's life were planted like a posthypnotic suggestion in my imagination. They did conjure up a sense of the near-foreignness of that nation, though not the deeper sense of absence in myself as an American that I would cross the border to explore.

Since moving from New England to Arizona eight years ago, I have experienced a profound change in my senses of both nature and culture. Living in the West has made me feel more intimately connected with the power of the continent as it reveals itself with such naked intensity in the desert, and with the wounded history that has shaped its landscape and people. In New England, the past has been paved over, beautified and made genteel. In the Southwest, the landscape tells stories more openly; they can be read along the Mexican border, on the urban Yaqui reservations and rural Hopi mesas, in the layering of cities over the bones of people who inhabited the continent for ten thousand years, and in the unremitting heat that cannot fail to open the collar of the most buttoned-up Easterner. The West has taught me that no matter the dominance human beings try to enforce over one another and the planet, the land is the final authority determining our destiny.

Living in the West has taught me that the political demarcation of the Mexican border is arbitrary and has nothing to do with the affiliations of nature and culture that define the region. My first excursion into Mexico, beyond the usual dismal and harried border forays to Nogales and Juárez, came while I was editing *Poetry of the American West,* an anthology for Columbia University Press. I wanted that work to speak about people's relationships with the West both before and after the Conquest, and I wanted to include the earliest written poetry I could find from the region. I decided to include some of the Aztec flower songs compiled in the sixteenth century by the Franciscan friar Bernardino de Sahagún. Although the majority of the Aztec and pre-Aztec scroll texts were destroyed by the Spanish, several friars with the assistance of indigenous informants preserved an astonishing body of testimony regarding the ancient cultures of what is now Mexico. The decision to include this work in the anthology marked an imaginative commitment to erase the border, to consider citizens of both nations simply as Americans. I do not mean to minimize the violent realities of the border. It would take far more than an act of imagination to erase the daily suffering that occurs there. However, once I had made that step as an editor, I began to wonder what else Mexico might teach me about what it means to be an American.

On my first extended foray, I spent a week sailing among the uninhabited islands in the Sea of Cortés. One day our boat approached a hunk of rock that looked about four acres in area, though scale can be deceptive in the shifting tropical light of the Baja. What is fact and what reflection become lost as islands mirage in and out of view. A boat may float in space beyond the edge of the earth, or an island in minutes may double in size, then melt to nothing. It becomes so hard to believe your eyes that you do not bother, instead accepting whatever reality drifts into view and then letting it go. But this island was real—a sloping bluff midway between Isla San Francisco and the southern end of Isla San José. On maps it is called Isla Coyote, but the locals call it Pardito. From a distance it looked like nothing more than a brown ledge with a couple of white gulls sitting on it. But as we grew near, the gulls grew larger and turned into small cupolas topped with lean black crosses.

Rounding to the western shore, we saw a crowded settlement of a dozen or so houses tucked into the lee of the rock—some scrap shacks with thatch roofs, the newer ones with corrugated fiberglass, one house of mortared stone with a wide veranda, finely made, three large metal water tanks raised high over the habitations, a photovoltaic panel, a tiny church and a one-room schoolhouse, its cinder-block exterior painted with murals depicting orcas and coral fish. Along the beach was a bouldered breakwater where lines had been strung and split fish hung to dry. One hurricane, I thought, and it would all be gone.

A panga slid up close to where we had moored some good distance offshore for lunch—two men and a young boy riding in the flat-bottomed boat powered by a bright new seventy-five-horse Yamaha outboard. We chatted about the weather, the bad fishing during the full moon, the price of the motor and where we were from. One said that he lived on Pardito; the other that he was born there, but now lives in La Paz and only comes on vacation to help his relatives or to visit. They could not agree on how long people have lived on the island. One said fifty years, the other a hundred. They invited us to go ashore.

Not wanting to invade anyone's private space, I headed up the foot-worn trail past a big *cardón* cactus that wore a shark's jaw strapped to its waist. Midway up the bluff above the cluttered houses stood the tiny white chapel. Climbing up to see what kind of place it was, I found a sanctuary ten feet square with a homemade altar of blue ceramic tiles on which rested a dime-store portrait of the Virgin of Guadalupe decked with fake gilding and roses, votive candles, a tiny cross of sticks lashed with blood red yarn, a photo of a blond woman sitting on a sailboat with a coffee mug in hand—a stout, ruddy, middle-aged woman—looking cheerful and relaxed. Dusty bundles of plastic-wrapped imitation flowers were stacked in a corner. The walls were painted sea blue and were peeling, the little room like a drifting bit of sea, except for the smell of wax and the soot staining the ceiling above the altar—the candle smoke from many necessary prayers made by people who relied upon the mercy of the sea. I'm not Catholic—cannot say I'm really even Christian—though I have experienced the presence of God enough times to say I'm a believer. It seemed wrong to be in such a place and not honor what it was made for. I knelt and said a prayer of my own, surprised at my sudden piety and need.

Stepping back out into bright day, I saw in the distance sheets of misty rain drifting out from the mountains in the west toward

Pardito. Snagged by the peaks on the mainland peninsula, storms rarely reach this little refuge in the sea. The tenor of the day had drifted too, now that my own inner need had connected with the foreign ground of the island. Descending the steep slope from the church, I passed packed bunches of houses, clotheslines hung with dusty chiles, a basket of garlic heads on the stoop, a salting shack where bins of fish were set to cure. The residents were hospitable and eager to chat, though I never stopped feeling that I didn't belong there. A local woman named Beatríx sat on the veranda railing of the one tourist house on the island. She told me the story of the blond woman whose photo I had seen in the chapel. For six or seven years the Californian couple had come on their boat to visit Pardito. The women had become friends. "There was love between us," said Beatríx, touching her heart, "like sisters." Her eyes followed a panga offshore where men were diving for clams. Her friend, she said, had been in a car accident in San Francisco, her leg badly injured. Medicines had hurt her heart, she said, and she had died at only fifty-eight. But her ashes were here, some of them, in a box beside her photo on the altar.

A group of men, four or six—someone was always coming from or going to the salting shed—worked at a rough wooden boning table on the beach. A man with a barrel belly wore a rubber apron, cartoons inked on his chest, a stitched surgical incision and a caricature of his face stubbled with whiskers. He sharpened a wide-bladed knife with water on a stone, then cut off the fins and gutted a thin skatelike fish he called *angelita*. Another man sliced out the backbone and filleted the meat with sure and careful strokes. He had made these simple cuts many times and he made them well.

We traded some provisions from our boat for fish and clams—sierra fillets and big chocolaty Colorado clams that the men said would be good for making seviche. "But you have to eat it with beer," one guy joked, "or else the seviche gets stuck in your throat." We asked if diving for fish was dangerous and did they worry about sharks, which are prevalent in the area. They shrugged, as if to say that it was just a thing they did. Another worked on the clams, splitting open the shell with a broad knife, cutting loose the meat, washing it in a plastic soup bowl with seawater, then cutting out the darker parts, washing again and dicing the white-and-orange segments. Deep blade marks inscribed every inch of the table's surface. Another man told me that sierra was good for a hangover. We laughed. He gave me a knowing look and said, "Yes, you have a few beers and at first you're happy, then you get sad."

Others loaded a panga with burlap sacks of clams, getting ready to ride forty miles to La Paz for a wedding. Beatríx was among them, wearing a bright orange short-sleeved blouse and khaki shorts. She smiled and waved as the panga pulled out. Everyone waved, those on shore and those setting out to sea, a gust of eager friendliness blowing through the whole village. It made me realize that though there are many things the people of Pardito do not have, they do have the experience of community, of being *in place,* something we keep looking for, feeling out of place in our dense, frenzied, glittering life of cities. And then it was our turn to leave, and we did so very slowly, watching a magnificent frigate bird rising over a nearby reef, carrying a fish so big it could barely fly.

"Religious man," wrote Mircea Eliade, "sought to live as near as possible to the Center of the World," a fixed point that was "an absolute reality, *the sacred,* which transcends this world but manifests itself in this world, thereby sanctifying it and making it real." The farther history proceeds, the farther it moves from that absolute, the divine source of life's upwelling, and the greater our nostalgia for the past. Visiting a place like Pardito where people still live in primary relationship with nature, closer to that mystery of origin, can satisfy an experience seeker's hunger only briefly. The appetite soon returns. I cannot deny for long that I live not at the center, but on edge, lost in a centerless sprawl where one reality abrades against another. And the more at odds I feel with my self-devouring culture, the more I long to leave again, searching for evidence of another way of existence, for a new experience that will make the world real again.

What's missing is not something that existed in the past or might come to be in the future, not something to be found on the remote edges of civilization or at a geographic center. What's missing is a connection with the hidden quality of existence that announces itself as spiritual. It is not something locatable, though seekers look for it in every place. It is a force that has been on the planet ever since humans climbed out of the trees, since the trees sprang from the ground, and maybe since the ground and water teemed with microbes. Perhaps it is a quality inherent in matter: to be embodied in a form is to harbor that memory of formlessness that we call spirit. Certainly it is a force inside the mind, one that keeps reawakening the hunger, not for things, but for the part of experience that has been denied. For it is a fact, as David Abram has written, that "phenomena can be hidden not just within the past or the future, but also within the very thickness of the present, itself—that there is an enigmatic, hidden dimension at the very heart of the sensible present, into which phenomena may withdraw and out of which they continually emerge."

Days and weeks may pass during which I am occupied with business, duty and repairs. I do not experience these periods of time. I do not know them. I merely move through them like an overtired traveler on a cross-country bus. The bus speeds past cities and towns, each of them melting into an indistinguishable blur. Then in my mind there may occur a glimmer, a momentary bridging of synapse—some memory, desire or insight—a thing intangible that becomes more real and durable than the scenery flying by the window. I will hold that intangible otherness for a long time, knowing it, drawing strength from it. Then when I look out the window again, say, at some cottonwoods lining the curves of a distant stream or a stand of chollas with spines catching the sunlight like a halo, I find that the scenery too has become real, that quality of innerness awake in everything. How private the most civilizing moments can be: in harmony with the world I *imagine,* I am in harmony with the world I *live.*

chapter 2

Beachcombing the Desert

I'm perched on a red conglomerate rock on a sloping rise above the northern shore of Isla del Espíritu Santo, one of the remote and arid islands off the coast of La Paz in the Sea of Cortés, a meadow of wild daisies and yellow flowering brittlebush surrounding me. Approaching the island on a forty-three-foot chartered sailboat, after hours of scanning striated cliffs topped with scrappy desert scrub, I had begun to expect that if these smudges of land had a story to tell, it would be one in which the only characters were rocks, and the plot one of geologic conflict and resolution. I had not expected this profusion. The suede of my hiking boots is coated electric yellow with pollen. Sticky leaves and stems are plastered knee-high to my jeans. The flowers stretch out in a pathless meadow, white and yellow freckles, purple trumpets of morning glory and nightshade, half a dozen other delicate beauties I cannot name. Here and there a *cardón* pokes up, its new growth graced with a crown of red spines. The smell of daisies, like pungent chamomile, blows up on the breeze. I step from stone to stone, crossing the flood of flowering.

These islands are among the driest in the world. One of the things I've come to love about desert places is their nakedness, how forms and patterns written on land nearly barren of vegetation remind me that for all the troubles and joys of being human the planet is primary. Fifteen million years ago the Sea of

Cortés did not exist. The Baja Peninsula was attached to mainland Mexico, most of which was under the Pacific Ocean. Then
the San Andreas fault opened, a splinter of land cracked away
from the continent, a gulf formed, and the ocean poured in. The
spreading continued until the earth's crust stretched and broke
into tumbling blocks, lava flowing up through the cracks. The
twenty-nine or so islands scattered along the eastern coast of
Baja California are less than five million years old—upstarts in
geologic time—products of the ongoing tectonic activity along
the fault, stark monuments to the forces that compressed, tilted,
cracked and spewed them into being. From a distance, they look
faded and colorless, like fabric left out in the sun too long.

I head down the slope toward the beach. A channel of aqua-
marine water snakes between protruding spits of land that nearly
meet, one fingering out from Espíritu Santo's northern shore,
and the other extending south from its near neighbor, Isla Partida. It's a graceful arrangement the land and sea have made over
the years. These two islands were one until a volcano erupted between them, leaving a crater that filled with the sea. On both islands, bluffs rise abruptly a few hundred feet inland—ragged
hills of banded stone, honeycombed tuff, nippled volcanic vents,
here and there a crease where a lush vein of saltbush and cacti
marks the occasional passage of water.

Both Espíritu Santo and Partida are uninhabited, except for
transient fishcamps built from beach scrap and plastic tarps.
Fishermen set up on the beach for a few days to hand-line or
spearfish, then head back in their pangas to the market in La
Paz. Ahead on the spit are three camps, one a skeleton of poles
and tattered fishnet, the others shingled with rusty corrugated
sheet metal, rotting plywood and cardboard, the mess tied together with fishing line. Several corroded refrigerators lie on the
beach, flat on their backs, along with a wheel rim used for a fire

grate, weathered work tables and benches slapped together from driftwood. Old bed springs, stack of tires, peanut can, broken crab trap, driveshaft, desiccated spiny blowfish, cracked brown clamshells litter the gravel. A driveway of sorts has been built on the beach—a twenty-foot span where red stones have been piled into little jetties forming a smooth pathway for dragging ashore the flat-bottomed pangas. The fishcamp is built out of rough necessity. I wonder what the men who fish here want for their futures, whether their lives seem difficult to them, or simply what they do.

In the slinking channel three brown pelicans stand on one sandbar, two great blue herons on another. At the tideline—a heap of thick oyster shells, hunks of pumice, bleached vertebrae—a turkey vulture slowly dismembers a fish. I get within a dozen feet before it glances up, dismisses me as no competition, and gets back to work. The beach is crawling with crusty two-inch beetles that dart away in all directions as I approach. Two oystercatchers are stilting around at the water's edge, their long scarlet bills brilliant in the afternoon's waning light, their dove-like gurgles enticing me, so I get down on my knees and creep closer. The light thickens to gold as the sun lowers and the breeze quickens off the water. I'm a thousand miles from anyone I know, idling on a desert island where I can't name half the plants I see, and I'm down on my knees before two birds that make me so happy to be alive I could weep.

Only six mammal species, most of them rodents, live on this desolate island. The closest thing to a charismatic megafauna is the melanistic black jackrabbit. Geographically isolated and among the most pristine on Earth, these islands are home to a large number of plants and animals that have adapted to these particular conditions and exist nowhere else. So localized is this biota that Ted Case and Martin Cody, who have conducted extensive research on the biogeography of the islands, report that 25 of 167 plant species on Espíritu Santo occur on no other Sea of Cortés island. The islands are also more sensitive to ecosystem decay than larger land masses, because extinctions are not replaced by immigration, nor are niches sufficient for new species to develop locally.

Much of the natural community exists here as it has for thousands of years, though human history has taken a toll. The Baja Peninsula was discovered by Spanish mutineers on board *La Concepción,* an exploring vessel dispatched by Hernán Cortés in 1533. Twenty or so rebels murdered their captain, took over the ship, and landed near what is now La Paz. Most were killed by the natives, but survivors told tales of abundant pearls. Cortés established a short-lived colony there. Several later exploratory and colonizing missions ventured as far north as the head of the gulf where the mouth of the Colorado River opens into the narrow sea. From there, explorers moved upriver in longboats as far as Arizona's Gila River. While early European settlers praised the thorns of the barrel cactus because they made such excellent toothpicks ("one of them will serve many years without repointing or resharpening"), pearls were the most compelling natural resource. The heyday of pearling from the mid-sixteenth to late seventeenth century nearly destroyed the local oyster population.

The first important plant survey was conducted by I. G. Voznesenskii, a preparator at the Zoological Museum of the Imperial Academy of Sciences, St. Petersburg. Case and Cody report that the Russian colony in Sitka, Alaska, depended on salt purchased in the Sea of Cortés for preservation of furs. They sent a ship to Isla Carmen once every three years. In 1841, Voznesenskii was aboard such a ship when it landed on Christmas Day. By February 4, he had collected 360 plant specimens of 113 species, which are currently held at Komarov Botanical Institute in Leningrad. More recently, in 1940, a celebrated marine exploration of the area was conducted by E. F. "Doc" Ricketts and John Steinbeck aboard the *Western Flyer*. Steinbeck's *The Log from the Sea of Cortez* is a classic of natural history writing and personal memoir, as well as a carefully documented scientific survey of the region's marine species. The trip also provided fodder for his story "The Pearl," based on a famous Baja legend.

Indian pearl divers, as the legend told, had been convinced by Spanish missionaries to donate the first pearl of each day's catch to the Blessed Virgin. One diver harvested such an outstanding black pearl on a dive near Cabeza de Mechudo (Head of the Long Hair) that, under the influence of the Devil, he neglected to make the offering. On his next dive, he didn't surface. When his companions searched, they found him dead, his leg caught in a giant clam, his long black hair waving in the undertow, his eyes ablaze with eternal damnation.

In the 1990s, fisheries in the Sea of Cortés have been depleted to near extinction. The sea now loses more water from evaporation than it gains from freshwater inflow, because of the diversion of the Colorado River to feed the urban and recreational needs of southern California and Arizona. The seawater's salinity continues to increase, endangering biota in the gulf. And the isolation that has protected the islands' fragile species is eroding now that a jetport serves La Paz and a highway runs the length of the Baja Peninsula.

In the thick light of dusk, I inch out the spit toward the oystercatchers. I'm on my knees whispering to two magnificent birds, trying to convince them they don't need to fear me, when a human song comes floating across the water. Two men are poling their panga off the shore of Isla Partida into the shallows. I can't make out the words, but the singer is belting them out with the abandon of one lost in passion. I could not live here, would starve from isolation. But to visit is to touch the spirit of the planet, to forget about grieving or longing, to be complete in the day's abundance. The late sun fans down through the clouds in a pattern like the radiating bars on a scallop shell.

The next morning, leaving the channel to head north, I look back at the daisy meadow as it quickly becomes a splotch of pale green—all its dimension and detail of whites, yellows, pinks, lavenders dissolving—a tiny blemish of no importance on a complex body of gray-brown rock. Ahead on Partida's shore stands another string of fishcamps as ragged as the last, except for one on the end that looks new, with siding painted yellow, a fancy boat driveway not made of heaped stone but finely worked by a mason, and in the backyard a bright blue portapotty marked, in Spanish, *Dames*. Not a slapdash camp built for work, this has the look of a vacation cottage. It marks a significant change in people's relationship with the place—a change from work to play. Here, as in countless regions of the world, the elemental experience of harvesting what one needs from the wild is on its way to becoming another blur on the horizon.

El Embudo is a deep narrow cove on the northwest side of Isla Partida. Like the twelve other sandy coves denting the western shores of Espíritu Santo and Partida, it was formed by the relationship between water and land. The rock strata of both islands tilt downward to the west so that rainfall runoff has worn arroyos by cutting from the heights to the coast. Below sea level the land has subsided, the mouths of arroyos becoming coves that eventually became lined with coral sand beaches. The east-west alignment of the arroyos means that every beach faces the spectacular sunsets that hang over the mountainous coast of the mainland peninsula. The coves provide welcome shelter for a few fishermen, kayakers, yachts and tour boats, though they are not all deep enough for protection from the Corumuel winds that blow up in the evenings. Pale sandstone walls edge El Embudo, bouncing sunlight onto the water so that it glows a luminous turquoise, as if lit from beneath. Gulls' underwings take on the hue as they fly over the water, looking like some rare species related to the blue-footed booby.

In the desert, one finds the way by tracing the aftermath of water—a winding density of desert willow or mesquite, pleasing curves cut in sand where water once found its way, a gouge eroded to form canyon walls. The arroyo at El Embudo cuts inland through a red-bouldered tumble, climbs uphill past a scattering of brittlebush and mangrove starts. No water passes down the drainage, but dragonflies circle over several small *tinajas* where stagnant rain has pooled. Legging up boulders as tall as my shoulders, slowed down by the work of it, I begin to see what's here—a beautiful turquoise-banded collared lizard lodged in a cleft, a micro-fern in the shade of an overhang, tiny fleabane blooming in a crease, mammillaria cacti, like fuzzy stones, growing where I can't spot even a crack in the rock, an elephant tree sprawled out on a ledge—anywhere a speck of soil has lodged some unruly life-form has taken root, sucking up water quickly when it's available and doing without month after month. The area gets about two inches of rainfall a year, most of it in the summer months. Some years there is no rain. By February things are usually pretty burned. But this has been a wet year, because of the trouble caused in the Pacific by El Niño, and the desert has responded with a green glow and profuse wildflowers, the seeds of which may have lain dormant for years.

Often here I've felt humbled by my ignorance. It's not that I need remedial training in plant identification. I can tell "pinnate" from "palmate" as well as the next amateur naturalist. But this area is incompletely explored biologically, because of its isolation, the harshness of its desert conditions, and the high degree of endemism. Of the 120 species of cactus living on the islands, half exist nowhere else. And though it is frustrating not to know the names of things I'm seeing, I've begun to appreciate that my ignorance makes me pay closer attention. When I identify a plant, I write "ocotillo," "blackfoot daisy" or "Mormon tea" in my notebook and move on. When I don't know what I'm looking at, I stop, draw a picture, make notes about the conditions in which it grows—the oiliness of the leaf, the redness of the petals, yellow of the seedhead, its volatile scent. In terms of sensory participation, I feel that I know what I don't know more fully than I know what I know. Perhaps that's why traveling to a new and unknown place is such a pleasure.

I pull up over a ledge and face a lush leafy tree, its pale gray trunk pouring out of a cave as if it had taken root in the earth's core. As the trunk emerges, it bends to climb into the light, tentacles and stilts reaching down the cliff to anchor the tree and drill for moisture. The wild fig has such a plastic relationship with rock—seeping out of a fissure, pasted against a cliff, oozing along a narrow ledge—that it ought to be called the rock fig. One can estimate the time that passes between floods in the arroyo—water so violent that boulders tear through the passage ripping out even such determined flora as this—by the age of the fig trees. Almost liquid in the way it has shaped itself to its circumstances. Almost liquid, too, the song of the canyon wren that fills the arroyo—first a rising, then a cascading twittering fall.

The ground levels to a high sloping hillside of chalky igneous rock, scattered with pocked boulders that look like something dropped by space aliens. One stands twice my height, a hollowed partial sphere, balanced on a lip so that I can stand inside to survey its inner surface, pitted, where bubbles of lava once popped. Sparse prickly pear crowned with yellow blossoms, gnarly purple-skinned cholla erupting with brown buds, pint-sized red-spined agave, and the richly green *cardones* standing sentry over the scrub—the colors of the living so radiant against scree, crusty ashflow, crumbled tuff, gravel remembrances where water has drained.

By the time I arrive at the summit's grassy plateau, I've forgotten the dry lake bed I climbed up here to see, so taken am I with the little grove of elephant trees poking up in a field of low yellow daisies. The papery succulent trunks branch out horizontally, not vertically, so that the tree with its pinnate leaves has grown four feet wide, but no taller than my knees. A few lavender butterflies circle over the brittle leaves. There's nothing to nectar on; perhaps they will lay eggs on the twigs and the tree will provide the first food for their larval offspring. I dig my nail into the bark to release the scent of its pungent oil.

What *did* I come here for? Certainly not simply to learn a few new words for describing wild things. Not simply to rack up on my abacus another of the last wild places. Not simply to renew my attentiveness to what surrounds me by moving to someplace new. I came here for some complicated combination of these three things—to fall in love again with the planet's power and mystery, to honor it by finding a language adequate to convey how absurdly lucky we are to share our moment in evolution's long clock. I came here to make my head a kind of microclimate where enthusiasm and hope might grow.

And I came here to stand on the edge of a hundred-foot cliff that marks a major fault line and to overlook a dry lake bed below that sprawls a mile or two wide. At some point in time, the headwaters of a stream ran up against the cliff, and water backed up to form a lake. What remains is a green meadow with a few snaking curves of drying water, rust-tinged seeps lined with rushes, discontinuous rivulets, yellow-speckled clusters of daisies, finer speckles of white and lush acres of grass—a tapestry over which the wind pours, hitting the cliff and gusting fiercely up to the ledge where I perch among clambering nightshade.

I finish drying my boots and socks in the wind as dusk begins to settle and gray storm clouds pile up over the gulf. I have lounged for hours on this precipice, have been visited by hyperactive lizards, cruised by a turkey vulture and captivated by a tiny blossom with three waxy petals, the central one a tongue of yellow, fringed with purple veins. I'm tired and hungry and worried that the rattlesnakes will be waking from their afternoon naps to start feeding, so I head back, this time taking a quicker route along the upper lip of the arroyo, then dropping down a final steep ledge to the beach.

Kayakers have pulled up for the night, their three tents pitched in the northern crook of the cove—six gray-haired campers busy with gas stoves and plastic bags of couscous and dried beef. I apologize for disturbing them. A paunchy man with a white beard and wearing a whistle around his neck smiles and says, "The beach belongs to everyone." They've come from British Columbia, traveling together for a month. There's an easy flow among them as the three couples prepare meals from dehydrated stores. It took them two days to paddle out here from Tecolote, near La Paz. One day when the water was rough, a panga fisherman towed them to shelter. They complain about the trash the fishermen leave on the beach—tin cans, fish guts and human waste. When she learns I'm a writer, the woman spooning cocoa into her mug says, "You know what will happen to this place when your story gets published."

"Keeping a place secret doesn't protect it," I reply, "it just keeps its destruction a secret." But I too have my doubts.

These islands are jewels of botanic and geologic wonders. While the local economy can benefit from an influx of tourist dollars, the local ecology stands a good chance of being brutally upset. The islands of the Sea of Cortés are protected as part of Mexico's Biosphere Reserve. But the nation has few resources for enforcing protection, and its government is highly centralized in Mexico City. Planners in La Paz have proposed development of a gambling casino and resort on Isla del Espíritu Santo. The importance of the place to those of us from the overdeveloped North is its unique wild heritage, its lack of human civilization. Here we can believe for a moment that we are a small and benign species, that we have left no scars on the land. But for the locals, the place is where they must earn a livelihood. And in remote parts of Mexico, that is not an easy task. Those of us living at the center of prosperity may long for the edge, but those on the edges (those lucky, say, to make three dollars a day) want in.

"What if I write about the beauty of the place and how easily its delicacy would be wasted?" I ask the skeptical one. "Wouldn't that help to protect it?" She softens, but we all feel the fact that we may be experiencing the place as few others will, the pressures of population and development being what they are. The moon slides over the cliff, making the white sand, the water and our faces shine. We sit on camp stools around their folding table and share news of our travels—how one hiker today saw a salmon-colored rattlesnake curled across a narrow path two steps ahead of him. He stopped and waited. The creature let him pass, rattling only as it moved off into the rocks.

.   .   .

Moored in thirteen feet of green water off Isla San Francisco's crescent beach, I scan the sandy ocean bottom, spotting a colony of garden eels swaying in the current, fanning their tiny brown pectoral fins, tails buried in the sand. If alarmed, they'll retreat into their burrows. For now, waving like weeds, they comb plankton out of the water. In the jay hook of the island's south end stand three makeshift tents of blue plastic, a panga on shore, a dozen pelicans diving so forcefully that loud splashes punctuate the peace. Two men in a panga near shore toss out a bait net. The pelicans and men are here for the same reason—massive schools of herring that boil to the surface in skittering pools. Seven or eight frigate birds cruise high above. More pelicans arrive—fifty or sixty—some floating on the surface, others plunging in muscular dives. For thirty million years pelicans have spent their afternoons this way. This species of brown pelican has nearly disappeared from the Gulf of Mexico and much of coastal California, largely because of pesticide contamination and loss of habitat. Baja California is among the last habitats where they thrive.

On shore I'm surprised to find that the topography and soil are very different from Espíritu Santo and Partida, only a half day's sail away. Geologists guess that Isla San Francisco may be five million years old, whereas those southern neighbors may be as young as eleven thousand years old. That allows a lot of time here for rock and coral to be ground into sand. And it shows in the rolling sand dunes that spread back from the beach, then dip into barren salt flats where fishermen have dug evaporation pools for drying and collecting salt. The dunes are lush with devil's claw, coyote melon, and something that looks like sea heather. Ropy *pitaya agria*—"galloping cactus"—rises in snaky heaps and elephant trees sprawl. Nothing grows very tall here, and as the land lowers toward sea level, becoming more salty, nothing grows at all.

On the salt flats the sand is crusty and pocked with craters where bubbles have erupted and broken, with sinkholes a half-foot wide full of gnat-and-mosquito-infested beige water. Four rectangular ponds have been dug with shovels and hoes—no sign of machinery, only a few prints of bare feet. When salt rises to the surface and crusts over, the fishermen rake it out of the pond into glittering coarse-grained pyramids. The salt will be used to preserve fish at the camps until it can be hauled back to market in La Paz.

A bare rocky ridge follows the curving jay of the island's southern tip. Though it's only about six hundred feet tall, it looks mountainous against the flatness of the salt beds and the tiny fishcamp. I hike back across the dunes to climb up and get the high view of the place. Across the channel, sheets of rain are slamming down on the Sierra de la Giganta, clouds caught in the crooks of its jagged bony spine. The high point of the range reaches nearly six thousand feet, high enough to snag a lot more rain than these islands ever see. Here the weather is unsettled, fits and starts of showers, but mostly dry.

I cannot imagine a life without seeing. Why is it that a certain arc of sand, a certain angle of light, a certain blue-green hue of water can give such pleasure? The poet Theodore Roethke wrote, "In a dark time, the eye begins to see." I sometimes think that the dark innovations of poison and danger human beings have con-tributed to the planet make us see its rare, untrammeled beauty with a keener eye than if we'd been merely benign. During the early voyages of discovery, people traveled across vast wilder-ness to find strange and exotic islands of human habitation. Now we travel across vastly populated continents to find tattered islands of wildness. I suppose the pristine vista from the high point on Isla San Francisco would have given pleasure to a traveler at any point in history. But I suspect that at this moment its beauty is most bittersweet.

From my vantage on a granite boulder, I look over the narrow waist of San Francisco, where the salt beds lie between two arcing coves set back to back forming a delicate isthmus. Steep rocky bluffs rise beyond the salt flats, and beyond that stands the rippling green backbone of Isla San José, the largest island in the area, graced with a beautiful *cardón* forest and a mangrove swamp that cushions the coast like a downy comforter. The vista offers an unusual hyperbole of wildness—sea, mountain and desert all at once. Just when I'm feeling smaller than ever, my knowledge of the place so partial, inadequate to get this shifting beauty to stay still on the page, I'm called out of myself by a whistle.

I look behind me. A man stands on a high promontory and gestures toward the sea, pointing to his eyes, then again to the sea. I guess he's telling me to join him and look at what he sees. We stumble through a conversation with my halting Spanish. His name is Rogelio. He manages to get across to me, using gestures and whistles as much as words, that he and six others are camped on the beach. He points to the sea where a panga heads away from shore. His brother has gone out to where the water is "deep and shallow"—perhaps a reef—to dive for cabrilla. The fishing is not good now, he says, because of the full moon—currents are strong. Fish can see the nets. They'll camp here for four days, storing the catch in a rusted refrigerator packed with ice and salt. Then he'll return to La Paz for three days. He prefers it here—less noise. What will he do when he goes there? Look around, have some beers, and rest. He's twenty-eight and single, likes being free, at least until he's thirty. Below at the camp his campañeros cook in a pot over the campfire, a few bits of laundry drying on an elephant tree. Up here on the peak a few thin fragrant vines snake over rock. The sun glides down toward setting, rays slipping through the cracks in gray clouds.

A single kayaker has pulled up on the beach, pitching his tent in the dunes. A big steel-hulled fishing boat, another chartered yacht, and a tour vessel bringing passengers to dive with the sea lions and swim with the manta rays have all moored in the cove for the night. *"Es muy tranquilo—refugio,"* says Rogelio, when I ask why so many choose this place to camp. He and his friends like to talk about the tourists, he says; otherwise they bore each other saying the same old things. Yesterday a big cabin cruiser anchored in the cove, and the fishermen traded some of their pargo, a variety of snapper, for drinking water. The solo kayaker? All he did was eat, sleep and swim. They thought that was funny. Tomorrow I'll be the joke. I imagine that his story of the gringa sitting alone with her notebook in the middle of nowhere will benefit from some manly embellishment.

The sky is dark, and we can no longer see his brother out near the reef. Whatever shred of a path I followed to get onto the ridge has melted into the night. Rogelio walks on ahead, leading me down. He steps quickly over boulders and scree in worn flipflops, while I follow, skidding in hundred-dollar hiking boots. He offers to bring me a fish in the morning, if they catch any tonight. I thank him and shake his hand. It has the texture of a foot, tough and worked.

All that night I wake fitfully hearing one sound or another— the hum of the tour boat's generator, the splash of the pelicans, the buzz of a panga's outboard motor, party voices from the yacht, the gentle lapping of waves—a complex music signaling how close I am, here in one of the wildest places in the hemisphere, to all the tensions and possibilities of human beings living together as best they can with their complicated needs and differences. The night closes around our small, accidental community—strangers moored from rough weather in the safe embrace of the land.

chapter 3

The Edges of the Civilized World

I traveled to the Sea of Cortés with the landscape photographer George Huey and the skipper of our chartered yacht, a capable and amiable expatriate who liked to play "Sgt. Pepper's Lonely Hearts Club Band" with his morning coffee. The skipper said he felt like the Maytag repairman, because unlike most of his customers, George and I didn't care that much about the yacht's amenities. I did not try the snorkeling equipment, donned my bathing suit only once and found hiking boots to be the most useful items in my duffel. The vessel was simply our taxi from one cove to the next. We were primarily interested in gaining a sense of the flora and fauna of the islands and understanding what was unique to the natural history and local customs—at least what could be gleaned from a hasty tour, a paltry few guidebooks, sparse encounters with fishermen and tourists encamped on the beaches, George's photographic lenses and plastic sacks full of film, my blank notebooks and binoculars.

George favored the angular light of dawn and dusk, so he would take the dinghy to shore before sunrise, getting in several hours of work while I dallied on board with coffee, trying to tune out "Sgt. Pepper" while perusing field guides and the previous day's notes. In the afternoon we'd go ashore, hike up an arroyo flowering with sea lavender, prickly pear and wild fig, or perch on a coastal bluff recording particularities of wind and light on the water. While the larger islands near La Paz—Isla del Espíritu Santo and San José—kicked me into that alert state of reverie for which I eagerly trundle the wilds, nothing surprised me more than my response to Los Islotes.

Two steep-sided rocky outcrops joined by a reef, a bent archway cutting through the smaller of the two, these islets are smeared and dripping with the whitewash of frigate birds and pelicans. Blue-footed boobies preen in nooks of the high ledges, their cartoon-colored feet making George speculate, "What could be adaptive about that?" I tried to think of something. "Their feet blend in with the sky, so that sharks don't notice them when they float on the water." The theory seemed a bit far-fetched. A latticework light tower protrudes from the plateau on top of the larger islet, several ladders scaling the cliffs on the south side. The dominant species on this piece of land, for once, is not ours, but the California sea lion. This bifurcated hunk of rock serves as its rookery—the year-round home for some three hundred of the animals.

As we passed by, dozens of sea lions lounged on the rocks, the fur dark brown when they first climb up out of the water, then turning shades of gray and gold as they dry. A big golden bull reared up, his head thrown back, as he bellowed and bellowed into the sky. Most of the sea lions were sprawled out on rocks. The skipper said it was breeding season, but it looked like sleeping season to me. I saw a pair of them draped on rocks twenty feet above the waterline. The heftier of the two had a large scar on his back, perhaps from a propeller cut—the blank of black skin looking like a jagged cattle brand, the Bar-Z.

But the sea lions were not alone at Los Islotes. In addition to our sightseeing craft, a Special Expedition tour boat was anchored off the southeast point, and two Zodiacs filled with red-vested high-tech emissaries were off-loading into the water with snorkels and masks. A dozen or so were already dog-paddling close to the rocky shore. A few sea lions seemed to be swimming near them. The people kept their voices hushed, and a guide on one Zodiac leaned near his charges to give quiet instructions before easing them over the side. There was an air of tenderness and caution in their motions. But rather than sharing the eco-tourists' obvious reverence and joy as they moved in closer to the rocks, I found myself enraged and disgusted at the sight. Why so visceral a reaction on my part, I wondered, to people so passionate to be intimate with nature?

I had the same response one evening when we anchored alongside another charter yacht, this one loaded with six young professionals from Los Angeles who told us, with euphoria as hyped as if it had been drug-induced, of their encounter with a massive herd of dolphins swimming with purpose in the middle of nowhere. The Californians were amazed to see several hundred dolphins packed close together, arcing energetically in and out of the water as they made their way toward whatever notion of "destination" inhabits a dolphin mind. They launched their dinghy into the midst of the animal turbulence and were thrilled, they reported, when the dolphins began to play around their boat. Wanting to get closer to the wild thing from which they still felt separate, they suited up with snorkels, masks and fins and dove in the water. The dolphins scattered like mercury.

Why do people always have to push the limits? Why wasn't it good enough to witness the dolphins from a respectful distance that didn't disrupt the mission on which the animals were bound? Why the hunger to get closer and closer until the animals drew the line? But trying to play with dolphins seemed fairly benign compared to the ridiculous extremes to which commercial ecotourism has grown to meet the ever-escalating desires of thrill-seeking nature lovers. One now can make a supervised dive among black-tipped sharks in the Caribbean, kneeling on the ocean floor while the monstrous ones rip at a frozen ball of chum the tour boat has suspended over their heads. "Professional shark handlers" in the Bahamas hitch rides on the pectoral fins of tiger sharks while the paying customers gawk with wonder through their dive masks. Am I just becoming another loudmouth in a nation of cranks, or does this trend suggest that we look for somewhat more civilized ways to connect with the non-human wild?

A few weeks after my trip, I met a field biologist who works as a guide on Special Expedition tours, including swims with sea lions in the Sea of Cortés. I asked him why he thought people needed these encounters with animals. "It's not a need," he said, "it's a desire. They want to be approved of by another species. It's a kind of penance for all the wrongs we've done against animals." I took him to mean not any personal transgression against beasts, but a collective guilt and grief about the extinction of the bison, the passenger pigeon, and the countless lost species we meet only in the daily news. People hunger to be close to a non-human world, or at least to a place in the world where humans are benign. I asked him if he thought that the boatloads of tourists swimming with the sea lions at Los Islotes were invasive or disruptive to the animals. He said he didn't think so and recounted that the sea lions become quite friendly. The cows and pups will come out to swim with the visitors and blow bubbles around them. Mothers actually push their babies closer to the humans.

But I was not convinced that the practice was harmless. What about disrupting their reproductive cycle? What would the cows be doing if they weren't out swimming around with humans? What happens to animals who learn from such encounters that humans are harmless when hunters or powerboat joyriders come churning into their midst? And what about the ospreys, I hammered on, telling how I'd seen a string of twenty naturalist-led tourists make a landfall on Isla San Francisco and traipse directly up to the ridge where a nesting osprey did its best to protect a little airspace. "Well," he conceded, "there's not really any regulation out there." Ahh, I have my purchase on his attention now, I thought, though a more sober inner voice cautioned, There you go again, a loose-tempered poet mouthing off to a sober scientist, having nothing but questions to back up your case. My anger seemed out of proportion to the situation, until it made me realize that I was responding to something emblematic of our wounded relationship with nature, our species's imperialism—as if it were our goal to domesticate every habitat on the planet, to turn every wild creature into a safe and innocent expression of human desire: the Bambification of the wild.

I spoke with Luis Bourillón, a biologist who had lived for several years in La Paz leading natural history tours in the area. He said that the sea lions used to be hunted for their oil, but had not been for many generations. Consequently, they have no fear of humans and have been getting tamer and tamer the more they are visited. He confirmed that while the animals are protected, at least theoretically, as part of the Biosphere Reserve, there are no signs or guides on the islands, no patrolling or enforcement. He helped to develop guidelines that were distributed to dive shops in La Paz, but what people do is often the opposite of what the guidelines say. Nearly every day of the year, boatloads of people snorkel up to the rookery and climb on the rocks. Bourillón and other researchers observed the phenomenon from the lighthouse to see if the visitations caused any changes in the animals' behavior. Amazingly, they did not see any. But there have been attacks, particularly during breeding season when the males defend their territory. When the visits first began, the animals would nibble on people's flippers, perhaps to see how the rubber felt. Now they nibble on hands, legs and necks. Their teeth are very sharp. If a person startles and pulls back, they get cut. "These are wild animals," Bourillón cautioned, "and they are very strong."

Recently a juvenile elephant seal has been hanging around Los Islotes. These large mammals, which can weigh up to two tons, breed on rookeries on Baja's west coast, where the males compete for females. Young males who have not yet won a mate wander in their search, and, in this case, the juvenile has begun to court both sea lions and human snorkelers. He is sexually mature, but having no access to females of his species, he has begun to mimic mating behaviors on the species that is available. His rituals involve holding a partner, nibbling on the back and neck, and forcing her to dive. He is capable of taking a partner a couple of hundred feet below the surface, though as yet his passion for humans has not gone this far. Such an unexpected interaction would brand the lovelorn, misguided youth as a problem animal and it is likely that he would be destroyed, just as we deem it necessary to destroy the cougar who finds a jogger to be appetizing prey, or the grizzly who becomes too familiar with our domestic territory. Our misreading of wild animals as titillating playthings can go very wrong.

After mulling over for some time this strange interaction between the civilized and the wild, I began asking my friends what they thought it meant to be civilized. "To live in harmony with your fellow man," said one. "To live, like the animals, in harmony with the earth," said another. "Basically it comes down to Tupperware," said the third. "To drink from a silver cup when riding in a stagecoach," said one who'd been perusing the celluloid mythology of the Old West. Tohono O'odham poet Ofelia Zepeda said, "Our people don't really have a word for it. My mother just used to say, 'Keep your hair out of your face and don't be like the enemy.' " For centuries the word has been associated with the life of cities, with building communities and defending them against barbarians, with manifest destiny and domesticating the wild. But what can it mean to be civilized now when the perils of global warming, a heat-trap sky, shrinking wildlands, and cascading extinctions are waking us up to the idea that the earth is a global commons, the future of which is in our bumbling hands?

It seems obvious to me that to be civilized at this point in history must mean to set limits, to understand when our comfort and freedom exact too extreme a cost on the overall well-being of others and on the planet that sustains us all, and to understand that certain possibilities, such as rediscovering faith in humankind, depend on setting limits, just as our freedom of movement in cars depends on occasional red lights. If we could learn to see the entire webbed sphere of life on earth as the commons and ourselves as being responsible for maintaining its habitability, then citizenship would no longer be considered in terms merely of our local human community. Citizenship would mean learning to live in responsible relationship with all the people, plants and animals on Earth.

I suspect that a hunger for just such an experience of citizenship drives many of us to become tourists. We long to see foreign places and cultures, exotic flora and fauna. We long even more ardently to see those that are imperilled, because we don't want to pass up the last chance to see the (fill in the blank). We long to get close, as close as the zoom lens has taught us we deserve to be. We want to look around, observe local traditions and wildlife, take a few photos, and go home feeling that we have learned anew something about the world's complexity, beauty and trials. We want to discover our own innocence as reflected in a foreign place. With such good intentions, how can we see our presence in another's community as invasive or disruptive?

But ask locals what it is like to be on the other side of the tourist equation, and too often the word "tourist" becomes an expletive. Tourists swoop into town like a flock of gulls at the dump, and pretty soon the town starts to feel like a dump. What once was a history full of suffering, dignity and hard-won survival becomes a parody of itself—cowboys, Indians and mountain goats depicted on T-shirts and jockey shorts. Native ceremonial ritual with centuries of tradition to give it meaning becomes the latest three-minute show on MTV. Public land gets trashed and private land gets bought by outsiders, escalating property values so that locals can no longer afford to own or even rent a home. Rather than being the center of town, locals become a service class devoted to meeting the needs of visitors who have a very short attention span for the needs and problems of the place. Everyone knows that the passers-through, and probably even the new settlers, won't be there to help when the local fishery or pulp mill is shut down. Locals, even those who have wooed tourists, come to resent those on whom their economic well-being depends.

We who love to travel do not mean to harm the quality of other people's lives. We do not mean to contribute to the erosion of other creatures' land or other people's cultures. But human hunger is robbing the earth of its future. The rich rob the earth out of their greed, the poor rob the earth out of necessity, and those many of us in the economic middle flounder in despair and ambivalence. We simply are too numerous. Nevertheless our hunger to experience other places and ways of life does not abate. Our confidence that lives somehow more authentic than our own are out there waiting to teach us the meaning of life does not fade no matter how many strip malls and burger barns we find on our journeys. And the good that can come of travel continues to be real and enticing.

By the year 2000, tourism will become the world's biggest industry, according to predictions by the World Tourism Organization (a United Nations affiliate). One of the fastest-growing branches of the industry is ecotourism, a phenomenon that has evolved out of the popularity of wild and exotic places and the growing concern about environmental degradation. As more and more people have wanted to see big game in the Serengeti or the rain forest in Brazil, the travel industry has responded with bigger and more frequent tours. One industry estimate holds that four to six million Americans travel overseas for nature each year; nature tourists from Europe and Japan further swell the stream. The most popular destinations (according to a 1987 study) are Nepal, Kenya, Tanzania, China, Mexico, Costa Rica and Puerto Rico. I suspect that Brazil, Rwanda and the Galápagos would be likely candidates to add to this list in the nineties. And ecotourism is very popular within the United States; in 1989, there were 265 million recreational visits to the national park system alone. Many communities, from Alaska to Wyoming to West Virginia, in which natural resources are so depleted that logging, mining, ranching or fishing are no longer economically viable ways of life are looking to ecotourism as a future.

The *principle* seems wise. Promote educational trips aimed at increasing the tourist's appreciation of the natural world and local cultures, while making economic success dependent on the preservation of that very biological and cultural diversity. Cut down the rain forest and the tourists won't come. Bring the fat tourist dollar into lean communities and the global commons will stand only to gain. The old utopian conservation approach of closing off wilderness in order to protect it has largely given way to the belief that the better a wilderness is known, the less likely it will be destroyed.

But there are problems. Mass tourism, no matter what the intention, may hasten environmental degradation by adding further stress to natural resources, wildlife and cultural integrity. One former ecotourism leader, who left the field because of her disillusion with its promise, spoke to me of her concerns: huge resorts plunked down on the beach displacing local people; cruise ships dumping waste offshore; safari vans rushing cheetahs for photos; hordes of camera-toting invaders gawking and snapping shutters at tribal people as if at Mickey and Minnie Mouse.

In addition, the nature of ecotourism makes its economic promise a gamble. One needs to look closely at where the ecotourism dollar ends up. A World Bank study estimated that over one-half of gross tourism revenues in the developing countries ends up back in developed countries. And while many travelers may be seeking penance with the wild, the intent of others is less noble. "I remember," the former ecotour leader reported, "a French family at a rather questionable rain forest camp off the Rio Negro in Brazil telling me that they hated humidity, didn't like boat travel nor sleeping in hammocks but felt that they had to get a few photos of the Amazon before it was gone." Even if the revenue from such tourists does go into the local economy of a disadvantaged area, what happens to that place when the fad to acquire such memorabilia of the wild dies out and a new market takes tourists elsewhere?

The Ecotourism Society (TES) was established in 1991 to address some of these concerns. Its definition of ecotourism is "responsible travel to natural areas that conserves the environment and sustains the well-being of local people," emphasizing that responsible ecotourism addresses both ecological and economic concerns. TES is a valuable resource for international research and planning, and if its guidelines for travelers and tour operators were adhered to, ecotourism might indeed heal the ills of exploitation and trivialization that tourism can create, and integrate conservation with development. On a hopeful note, the tourism industry's market profile of an ecotourist is a person who is interested in making a contribution to conservation, is well educated, is an experienced traveler with disposable income, and tends to be "amicable," "broad minded," "intelligent," "self-assured" and "sociable." Such people, it seems reasonable to conclude, will do their best to make this kind of travel a virtue.

At a recent visit to the Alaska Raptor Rehabilitation Center in Sitka, I was reminded by a naturalist of the correct procedure for handling an injured bird. "Our first impulse," she said, "is to pick it up, bring it close to our faces, cuddle and talk to it. But that amount of visual input can terrify the bird so that its heart will speed up and it will die." The proper technique is to cover the bird's eyes, thus quieting its alarm prior to further handling. I cite this example because it illustrates so well how the results of our actions are not always as benign as our intentions—and Lord knows we have plenty of examples to suggest that this axiom might be a useful one. Given the inordinate human capacity for blindness to the consequence of our actions, how might we exercise more care when trying to get closer to nature? It is as foolish to think that our presence does not upset the behavior and metabolism of wild animals, as it is to think that tourists will not change the character of a community. If we don't know whether snorkeling up to the sea lion rookery will interrupt the animals' reproductive cycle, then why risk it? If we don't know whether tour boats chasing gray whales off the Baja coast will harm the leviathans, then why risk it? The same principle might be applied to cultural tourism in which travelers from uprooted cultures visit remote villages to gawk at "authentic" indigenous people.

Some of my "green" colleagues are fond of saying, "We must stop trying to control nature." But I have come to feel that such a position denies how powerful a force the human species is on the planet. We will control nature, often without even being aware that we are doing so. Sure, there will be microbes and hurricanes that will get the better of us. But we will find new antibiotics and better ways of predicting the atmosphere's surprises. If one has faith in the profound and mysterious process of evolution on earth, one must also have faith in the power that process has invested in us, as the dominant and determining species on the planet. One must also have faith in our ability to rise to the astonishingly difficult challenges we face in preserving the global commons.

Perhaps it seems absurd to think in terms of a global commons when we haven't yet learned how to be citizens of a human community without war, domestic violence, rapacious waste and the trivialization of suffering that currently passes for entertainment. I've always thought that if the world suddenly faced marauding alien imperialists from another galaxy who gave us a thirty-day ultimatum to stop our warring ways or else, we'd learn fast how to unify and protect each other. And we do face a common enemy capable of destroying the life we love on earth. As Pogo said during the Vietnam War, "We've seen the enemy and it is us." Suddenly we are both the invading barbarians and the only ones around to protect the city. Each one of us is at the center of the civilized world and on its edge.

. . .

After leaving Los Islotes, George and I talked about the work we do and wondered whether, for all of our good intentions and love of the wild, we were merely shills for the worst of the tourist industry, the harbingers of the hordes that would despoil the delicate islands we were privileged to see in their innocence. We talked about Robinson Jeffers, whose radiant poems celebrating the natural world became so misanthropic late in his life that he suggested nuclear war would be a good thing, because it would purge the earth of our ruinous kind. We talked about the idea of "eco-porn"—the way idealized photographs of animals may foster the idea that creatures exist for our pleasure, rather than for the inherent dignity of their own existence. Still, it's hard to feel anything but admiration for a man who gets up before the sun, lugging a heavy tripod and backpack up the side of a mountain, then waiting, and waiting some more, for the light and the wind to be exactly right in order to hold on to a split second of the world's beauty. And it's hard to believe that my own attention to wild beauty is anything less noble than a healing of the soul. The human desire for wildness is strong and deep, because we feel so distant from that source and its unconscious movements in our bodies and minds.

But, given that the hunger for the wild too often means that we love nature to death, I began to wonder how else I might feed that hunger. I began to think about how, collectively, we who love to travel might be more gentle, more thoughtful, more willing to redefine what gives us a wild thrill. For one thing, we might look for and nurture what's exotic and wild in ourselves— our imaginations and complicated emotions. We might come a bit closer, physically closer, to the most terrifying wilderness of all, our own mortality, the awareness of which makes us unique among animals while at the same time making us equal to all creatures that suffer birth and death. To understand our own animal nature, we might sit at the bedside of the dying or attend the birth of a child.

For another thing, we might understand that our hunger to be thrilled and frightened by nature's fierceness suggests our need to be humbled by the powers that have given us our lives. We might abandon the notion once and for all that we can know the world as it might be without human presence. This might lead us, when we travel, to be interested in what is at stake for local people in their relationship with their place, and to experience some exchange other than a monetary one. We might soften our alienating presence in another's community by traveling alone or in small groups, by having a single leisurely conversation with a stranger who has nothing to sell us. And we might be certain that the money we spend as tourists, especially when we visit economically deprived places, goes to those who most need it, rather than to the glitzy corporate resort that employs locals as parodies of a dying way of life—waiters and maids dressed as their peasant ancestors, while the resort's very construction may have displaced the last remnant of a local peasant culture. We might decide not to visit the most popular nature tour sites, or those where delicate conditions would be harmed by our presence. Rather than going and taking a snapshot, we might stay home and send a check. We might improve our position in the biological community by informally apprenticing ourselves to another species, slowly developing a deep understanding of one small corner of the biological world as an antidote to the overwhelming tide of superficial information about everything on earth that threatens to drown our imaginations.

These are not prescriptions for what we should do to save the world. I don't know what we should do. I do know that my sense of urgency about protecting the world's beauty and bounty has grown too keen for me to offer merely poetic ambivalence, or despair, or yet another plea to write to Congress. Perhaps, as Audubon once pointed out, it is not the world that needs saving, but our character.

After leaving the Sea of Cortés, I traveled, as an ecotourist, to the Mexican state of Michoacán to visit the monarch butterflies. There, on five forested mountaintops, the entire population of monarchs living east of the Rockies spends the winter. They migrate from as far away as Ontario, and though not all of the hibernating animals will live long enough to remigrate back to their starting place, some will. The feat seems even more heroic when one learns that the migrating individuals may be two or three generations removed from those making the previous trip from the north. The monarch migration is one of the most impressive natural phenomena on the planet. And the monarch reserve, established in 1986, is one of the more successful ecotourism sites.

The area to which the monarchs migrate is poor, having been farmed by local residents living for centuries on steep, now largely deforested hillsides. It looks a bit like a peasant California—rolling grassy hills, a few peaks topped with evergreen forest. The homes are mostly adobe, ramshackle, except for the care shown in the hanging planters made from aluminum cans that deck the outside walls. Fencerows are marked with agaves farmed for making tequila or pulche, a fermented drink with a nasty reputation. Cornfields are worked with oxen, children and hands.

Until one has experienced walking in a wind caused by flapping butterfly wings, it is difficult to convey the power of the monarchs' aggregate presence. Millions of the animals are packed into the trees, hanging like huge colonies of mistletoe, or sacks of laundry. On warm days, many will flutter loose from the mass, the air becoming a blizzard of delicate, papery bodies, as they lower to sip water from a pool or nectar on wildflowers dotting the forest floor. It is the largest gathering of a single animal anywhere in North America. They will live through the winter by metabolizing stored fat. So rich are these fat bodies that if this forest were to burn, the trees would flame like whale-oil lamps. Those monarchs fluttering to the flowers in midwinter are ones whose fat supply is too low to sustain them. They are unlikely to survive the cold. The forest floor is carpeted with dead monarchs. This is their sanctuary and their mortuary.

Of the five protected sites, only two are open to tourists, and these only under the guidance of *vigilantes,* retrained loggers whose job it is to protect the forest from black market logging, disruption and noise. GUARDA SILENCIO read the signs posted along the trail—protect the silence. The remaining three sites will not be opened until naturalists, both U.S. and Mexican, have a better understanding of the impact of tourism on the butterflies. As the *vigilantes* led our group through the forest, they leaned down and swept the dirt with their hands in order to clear the path of animals that had fallen in our way and did not have the energy to rise. At first I thought the action was a superfluous ritual—the scattering of bodies on the trail looked dead. But then I saw a man take one of the creatures in his palms and blow on it with his warm breath until the wings loosened and the frail one staggered into the air.

We may not know yet the impact of tourists on the monarchs, but I can say a thing or two about their impact on me. I left that ground with a quiet sense of the holiness of what has transpired on this planet as it has transformed from a ball of flaming rock to all this living complication. In an open-air stall with a wood-fired cookstove, a sturdy woman with a braid that reached the back of her knees sold me a meal—*pollo con mole y tortillas azules y arroz,* the sweetest meat I'd ever tasted, flavored with marigold blooms fed to the local chickens to make their yolks more yellow and their flesh more fragrant.

Another woman pressed out handfuls of blue cornmeal—the primary crop grown on these steep depleted hills. She laid the dough between sheets of wax paper, flattened it in a wooden tortilla press to form the dark imperfect circles I would eat and eat until I could eat no more.

chapter 4

Annual Report

I travel every year to the island of Grand Manan because there my senses of place as geographic locale and mental habitat coalesce. I hold the island in mind during each long year of work and travel, calling it up when the nattering and fragmentation of daily obligations get me down, soothing myself with images of the refuge to which I will return for a few weeks in summer, as I have every year for the past forty or so. My allegiance to the place is not exactly an expression of national or ethnic identity, but akin to that. I know that my character has been formed in part by my relationship with its strong and craggy isolation, its inviting wilderness and its warm, earthy, hardworking people. I know too that it has instilled in me a sense of the land (and sea) as common wealth, by which I mean that the place is an investment in which everyone has a stake and from which everyone draws sustenance.

A Canadian island settled by Loyalists in the late 1700s, it has thrived for two centuries because its residents have taken their livelihood from the sea. The early weir fishing techniques practiced by settlers in the Bay of Fundy were learned from the Passamaquoddy and Maliseet people. In 1745 the English sea captain William Pote, captured by Indians on the lower St. John River and held for four months, wrote this entry in his diary:

This day as we was paddling up the river we passed a small cove and perceived at the head of it there was a salmon playing in the cool water at the head of the cove. We landed very carefully and cut bushes and brought them down to the entrance of the cove and while some of us was employed with perches and our paddles etc., thrashing the water to hinder the fish from coming out of the cove, the others built a ware across the entrance of the cove with bushes and our blankets, etc. and we caught in this cove fifty-four salmon which was so exceptable at that time that I shall never forget the joy I was filled with.

The weir fishery developed from such slapdash shoreline dams to today's graceful offshore structures, built with timbers and nylon twine, that snare massive schools of herring as they move toward the shoals. Fundy waters have been abundant with fish stocks, and islanders abundant in their resourcefulness at tapping the riches. Herring do not always frequent the same waters year after year, but the islanders have adapted well to the boom-and-bust nature of harvesting from the wild. The islanders' careful techniques for curing and smoking herring generated early market opportunities in Canada, the United States, Europe and the Caribbean. Sardine canneries have prized the fish caught in weirs because the method is gentle and keeps the meat intact. The island fishery has become both specialized and diversified. New techniques and fisheries have been blended with old—purse-seining, lobster trapping, scallop dragging, hand-lining, gillnetting and dulse harvesting each playing an important role in providing Grand Mananers both a solid livelihood and a sense of homemade pride. The health of the fishery has been synonymous with the health of the community.

On land the sense of common wealth takes a somewhat dif-

ferent form, but is nonetheless one of the characteristics that
defines the place. A trail system circles the island's perimeter,
passing along cliff edges above the Bay of Fundy's rips, eddies
and crosscurrents. These are volatile and potent waters with one
of the highest tidal differentials in the world. According to Mic-
mac legend, the god Glooscap departed the Bay of Fundy with
such a great splash that the water continues to slosh back and
forth to this day. Shipwrecks have been common, hundreds of
boatmen lost in the icy waters. The perils have taught island
men an attentive and serious manner, and have given the island
its cliff-clinging trails that were cut originally in order to search
for survivors along the island's steep, uninhabited western cliffs
in the days before Coast Guard ships and helicopters were available to perform the service. The hiking trails now are maintained
by a volunteer association and are used mostly for recreation.
They cover the entire circumference of the island, and cross a
good deal of its interior—nearly all private land, but no one
complains or puts up a fence, the general opinion being that if I
let you cross my land, then you will let me cross yours.

The same attitude pertains to nearly all of the island's beautiful places—the black sand beach at Deep Cove, the high granite outcrop of Beech Hill where wild blueberries proliferate and
a hiker can see most of the island's villages spread out below, the
remote grassy promontory called Hay Point near Southern
Head, or the Whistle (named for a foghorn that groans rather
than whistling) on the cliff near Long Eddy Point where anyone
might show up on any night to watch the sunset with whatever
improvised crowd of two or twelve shows up. These places are
not provincial parks, though there now are two on the island.
They are simply part of the common wealth belonging to who-
ever chooses to visit them and experience their value as beautiful places.

Those who are susceptible to greed for this kind of wealth can spot each other in a second. One day at the laundromat, where the wash water looks and smells like the island's interior bogs, I met a guy who was building a house in Seal Cove. He had been born here, but now lives in Nova Scotia, returning in the summers for carpenter work and for something harder to name, though I would like to call it love. "It's not place a person wants to let go of," I said. "Yes," he replied, "it gets into your blood." And I imagined the two of us as kids here picking up in our veins some peat-flecked substance that keeps circling through our fingers and brains, calling us back to its place of origin.

But this place, too, like so many remote communities, is on edge. As early as 1851, official warnings had been sounded about overzealous commercial harvesting in the area. The herring were then so plentiful in their breeding ground off Southern Head that no restraint seemed necessary. Thick layers of spawn covered net ropes and anchor cables; windrows of milt washed up on beaches. But in that year Moses Perley's "Report on the Fisheries of the Bay of Fundy" cited that the fishery "was continually falling, and would eventually be destroyed, from the reckless manner in which it was prosecuted, and the place being overfished." His work resulted in a seasonal ban on taking fish from the herring spawning grounds off Southern Head. The herring fishery continued to thrive, with some disruptions caused by natural fluctuation, for 150 years, while islanders also diversified their efforts into groundfish, lobster and scallop fisheries.

In the summer of 1993, three years after the cod fishery in Newfoundland had crashed, the New Brunswick Department of Fisheries and Oceans reported that the inshore groundfishery of the Bay of Fundy was on the verge of commercial extinction.

Stocks were low, particularly of fish mature enough to reproduce, growth was slow and a dangerously high percentage of fish
was being killed by the fishery, predators and ocean conditions.
According to the Conservation Council of New Brunswick, only
15 percent of an estimated 35,700 hectares of original Fundy
salt marshes remains; hundreds of acres of clam flats are closed
because of sewage contamination and toxic algae blooms; estu-
aries once supporting fisheries for scallops, lobsters and herring
are stagnant because of pulp mill pollution; acid rain and air
pollutants have damaged coastal forests as well as the phyto-
plankton that are essential to the marine food web. Fishermen
and government regulators do a tense and often hostile dance
around each another, trying to protect both a way of life and
the ecosystem that supports it. Everyone feels the tension of
knowing that change is necessary; no one knows what that
change will require.

Some islanders look to aquaculture to replace the traditional
fishery. But fish farming, in addition to producing new sources
of waste, is no less dependent on a healthy marine food web
than the weir fishery. Janice Harvey, in *Turning the Tide: A Citizens' Action Guide to the Bay of Fundy*, provides this illustration:

> *Two kilograms of feed are required to grow each kilogram
> of salmon harvested. To produce one kilogram of herring
> meal [the basis of salmon feed], five kilograms of live her-
> ring are needed. No live herring are allowed to be har-
> vested directly for meal; instead, herring wastes, including
> wastes from the roe fishery, are the source of meal. In 1989,
> one meal factory processed the equivalent of 30,000 tonnes
> of herring. To produce one tonne of salmon, an area of
> marine plankton is needed covering about one square kilo-
> metre of ocean, which then transforms into herring*

*growth. To produce 20,000 tonnes of salmon would re-
quire the plankton equivalent of 20,000 square kilome-
tres, an area roughly twice the size of the Bay of Fundy.*

In spite of the biological costs, salmon aquaculture is growing in the region. In 1993 the estimated harvest for the province was estimated to be worth $100 million. While Grand Mananers have established several small, locally run projects, the original vision of independently owned fish farms replacing other local fishing activities has not come to fruition. Large corporations, Canadian and Norwegian, run the most ambitious sites in the Bay of Fundy—vertically integrated industries with their own smolt hatcheries and feed operations, with automated feeding in the floating pens controlled by computers on land. This may make economic sense, but it is a far cry from the hands-on traditional knowledge of a small-scale fishery.

More than skills will be lost when the old techniques are no longer viable. I wish we believed that the rough-hewn beauty of a herring weir staked in the shoal beneath a rugged cliff is something that the world needs, because it is beautiful and locally grown, because men take pride in knowing how to do this thing that men elsewhere do not know how to do. I have watched men enter a weir in a dory, one leaning over the bow to lower a weighted line into the depths to feel for herring, the other man slowly working the boat along. They can sound ten fathoms down in a weir by this method, and, from the feel of the fish bumping into the line, estimate how many hogsheads might be harvested. I wish we believed that the art of sounding for herring with one's hands is something the world needs, because it shows how sensitive a man's touch can be. But these skills will go, as have those for bringing herring to the surface by torching the

water with faggots soaked in kerosene, or for treating cotton
weir twine in vats of hot tar before nylon was invented.

So much of what we learn is dispensable in the interest of
progress. And while it seems wise and necessary to exercise less
risk, less hardship, less blindness in our dealing with the environment, I wish we could slow down the bullet train of progress
in order to preserve skills learned by living and working in a
place, or at least in order to mourn the losses. A man on a salary
sitting at a computer monitor feeding salmon penned a half mile
away has less sense of ownership in his place and in his future
than a man working a dory inside a weir he has built by hand,
from which he will pull, if he is lucky, enough herring to get his
family through another month, another summer, another year.
The doryman may be less secure about his income, but he is in
touch with the currency of his place. But "the currency of place"
is a poetic idea and will not pay for the mortgage, the home entertainment center, or the winter vacation in Florida. The islanders want what people all over the world want, and who are
we, the affluent thing-mongers from the United States who
taught them how to want more and better stuff, who are we to
tell them that their forebears' modest ways of living really are
best?

Some islanders, encouraged by the provincial government,
look to tourism for an economic leg up on the future. In the
past few years a flurry of guest cabin construction has swept
through the island, a few whale-watching operations have begun
leading tours into the bay's right whale nursery, and a sea-
kayaking operation has been floated. But the place offers little
either to the linen-and-martini crowd or to the polyester-and-
Budweiser set. The island is strictly religious and does not con-
done such risqué entertainments as movie theaters and bars

(though one can rent the standard fare at several video stores and buy booze at the government liquor store sporting the highest sales figures in the province). The ocean is too cold to swim in, the beaches too rocky to sun on (not to mention the fog), and the tennis courts bear a surface as erratic as a potholed backroad. There are no upscale resorts, no classy marinas, no bowling alleys, no gaming arcades, no water slides or minigolf. In short, there is little on the island other than its natural assets (and the concomitant natural history museum, provincial campground and rugged trail system) to draw tourists away from the more popular Maritime pilgrimages to Cape Breton Island or Prince Edward Island. And finding a way to market unspoiled natural assets without selling them down the river is indeed a challenge.

No one has written more bitingly than Douglas Adams about the strange hopes found in far-flung places that tourism will stave off the Janus-faced perils of poverty and overdevelopment. In *Last Chance to See . . .* the author, who is better known for his comedic work *A Hitchhiker's Guide to the Galaxy*, compares the phenomenon to convergent evolution:

> *Exactly the same behavior pattern had emerged entirely independently on the other side of the world . . . the local people cheerfully offer themselves up for insult and abuse in return for money which they then spend on further despoiling their habitat to attract more money-bearing predators.*

Even for the good-hearted tourist who makes a pilgrimage to the last unspoiled places, the experience is often one of loss. For, as Adams writes, he finds that "the gifts he has brought with him from civilization turn to dust in his hands as he realizes that everything he has is merely the shadow cast by what he has lost."

. . .

When my family began coming to Grand Manan in the fifties there were no signs on the stores. They looked like houses from the outside; they usually were houses. The place was so small that no one needed to be told at this place you can buy tea and milk, at this one rope and nails, at this one aspirin and penicillin. No one needed advertising to lure customers, and competition did not seem to be a part of the commercial game. If you lived in North Head, you went to Harry Stanley's store for groceries; if you lived in Seal Cove, you went to McLaughlin's. The selection of goods was limited, particularly fresh fruits and vegetables. Those of us summer people from richer places would ply the stores from one end of the island to the other looking for a decent head of lettuce, often ending up with only a soggy turnip. Doing without added to the island's charm for us. Our favorite topic of conversation, to this day, is the comical adventure of satisfying our appetites on the limited resources the island offers. Some weeks the produce truck does not show up at all, and we pick lamb's-quarter from the beach for greens, sharing the bounty with neighbors. Some weeks the ferry breaks down and the danger of being shut off indefinitely from supplies sobers everyone.

When the big IGA store came to Woodward's Cove a few years back, with its corporate logo and streetside signboard promoting the weekly specials, some folks bemoaned the change— "It's the end of the island!" Several of the small village stores went out of business. But everyone is happy to have more choices in what and when to buy. In the summer of 1995 when a local landowner-turned-entrepreneur fenced off the path to the Hole in the Wall, a hiking spot along a section of the original trail system that is accessible enough to make it a favorite for locals

and tourists alike, I joined the chorus—"It's the end of the island!"

The short path to the geologic oddity had been blocked with
a homemade sign reading "Hole-in-the-Wall Park" that posted
fees for guided or unguided tours, along with the hours the
"park" was open. Fine, I thought at first, someone needs to make
a buck, but there are other access points to the trail entering
from land still considered public domain. So I headed for Swallow Tail Light, where the Red Trail edges the ragged coastal cliff
for a mile or two. A half hour into the balsam-scented woods, I
passed a little meadow of the late-blooming butter-and-eggs—
a wild snapdragon, introduced from Europe, that favors the
same waste places inhabited by wild currants and raspberries.
The hum of bees filled the air with the sweet music of their work.
A tweedy peregrine flew near. I was deep into the loveliness of
the wild and felt welcomed by the land—the place once again
had come to own me.

Then I rounded a bend, rose from a dark draw to face a two-
foot square of plywood painted with "Orange Trail Entrance to
H-I-T-W Park." The single-file path widened to a bare, scraped
woods road; tent sites had been bushwhacked among the
stumps; another sign directed the way to the toilets and parking
lot. I had unwittingly crossed the line separating the land as
commonwealth from the land as private property on which I
had no right to trespass unless I paid the requisite fee. Never before had the word "park" sounded like an expletive to me. I've
walked here all my life, I thought, as if that could justify my continuing to do so against the will of the owner. Don't get me
wrong—I love parks and I value the guided experience of the
wilderness that parks offer. A well-designed park cautiously
manages its natural assets, not for private gain, but in the interest of protecting the land as a community resource. It is no mere

happenstance that the best parks, whether in Canada or the United States, are sanctioned and run by government agencies. This is one of the good things our governments have done; they have preserved at least part of the natural heritage of our magnificent continent for present and future generations to experience. But a portapotty, a fee and a handful of signs do not make a park.

I knew my way well enough in those woods to continue on without risking being caught, though I admit I delighted in the fantasy of being apprehended, refusing to pay, getting arrested, spending the night in jail and subsequent days on the soapbox to defend the land as the commonwealth of all who love the island. The deeper into the woods I went, the more hokey things got. In a dense stretch of brushy hillside another sign was planted: "Treasure? Pit: 20 Paces East, 3 Paces South, Beware of Ghosts." A half hour farther on: "Haunted Forest: Are you sure you want to go on?"

It is all too easy to read change as doom. These changes do not mark the end of the island, but they do mark, for many people, a turn in our notion of the island as a mental habitat—its imagined innocence as a place unsullied by the commercialism and self-interest that drive so much of North American culture. Mistakes will be made in every human enterprise—and it *is* a mistake to diminish, as those inane signs attempted to do, the dignity of the wilderness and its capacity to educate the human soul. What troubles me is how often we read our mistakes not as opportunities for learning, but as prognostications of doom, further evidence that our species is a blight on the planet, that our coming extinction will be a kindness to whatever few species may escape our greedy subjugation. We don't have a lot of faith in ourselves anymore. Much of our astounding technological progress over the last few centuries has resulted in the fouling of our nest. And while human kindness may prevail in most neighborhoods and families, we are obsessed with the pathology and violence occurring next door. When most people speak about the future, it is with dread, not hope: "We're lucky to have lived when we did."

Most of us born after World War II consider ourselves lucky to have lived at all. The summer of 1995 marked not only the opening of a new "park" on Grand Manan, but also the fiftieth anniversary of the invention of nuclear bombs and their deployment by the United States against the cities of Hiroshima and Nagasaki in Japan. The season was ripe with media commentary and reflection. The director of the Los Alamos lab spoke of the pride felt in the invention of the weapons that not only ended the war but also have kept us from another world war for half a century. A man threw what appeared to be blood on the commemorative obelisk at Trinity Site, New Mexico, where the bomb first was tested. A scientist warned that nuclear waste stored in the catacombs dug into Yucca Mountain could reconfigure, sparking a self-sustaining apocalyptic reaction. A colleague refuted the danger, saying that the science behind the theory was not good. Experts debated about whether or not using the bomb against civilians had been necessary in order to subdue Japan's aggression. As I listened to these voices and thought about our lack of faith in our civilization, I began to appreciate the connection between the technology and the psychology of doom.

For over fifty years the terror of nuclear annihilation has haunted the human imagination, as have the very real images of the devastation and suffering caused by the atomic bombing of Hiroshima and Nagasaki. My generation—the "duck-and-cover" cohort—grew up in the fifties and sixties watching educational films designed with the hopeless task in mind of convincing children that the world was safe for them because nuclear weapons guarded the borders of their country. Of course, the very idea of borders became irrelevant when one studied maps of the nation showing primary, secondary and tertiary targets at which the Soviets had aimed their arsenals. No place was safe. It was small comfort that ever-new-and-improved weapons were similarly ready to fly toward our enemy. We talked about what would be worse—to die in a nuclear war or to survive one. We talked about what should be stocked in a bomb shelter—definitely birth control pills because no one would want to bring a child into that world. We talked about the families who had built shelters in their basements, little cinder-block burrows adjacent to the family rec room. My father said it made no sense to build one. He had studied the maps and said we would be in the firewave if Hartford was bombed—we would only bake. And the bombs spread like mold around the globe.

The purpose of nuclear weapons is to instill fear and terror. The need for the weapons is based on the assumption that humanity's dark side is so powerful it can only be controlled by a doomsday technology. This terror was well earned in the atrocities of a war that called into question what it means to be civilized. If Germany, as a culturally advanced civilization, was capable of the systematized evil of the Holocaust, then that nation's notion of what it means to be civilized had to be thrown out. If the United States, as the defender of civilization, had to depend for victory on the most barbaric weapons in the history of war, then our notion of civilization was darkly contaminated too. We have not recovered from these blows to our sense of purpose and well-being. As Francis Ponge put it, the century that was to be our greatest hope became that of our greatest despair. We have acclimated to the assumption that we are so violent an animal we need to hold the threat of imminent death over one another in order to continue to live.

Growing up, I did not believe I stood much chance of surviving into adulthood. I thought it very unlikely that the year 2000 would arrive with anyone around to witness it. In the nineties our attention has been subdued by modest progress toward nuclear disarmament. But as long as these weapons exist, we cannot claim that our children and grandchildren are safe from nuclear threat, that bombs no longer sleep in their earthen and submarine beds dutifully waiting to be propelled into service by technocrats or madmen. We can hardly claim that we understand what has happened to our psyches because we have harnessed the atom and aimed its destructive powers toward ourselves, or why we feel compelled to continue this practice, rather than finding a way out of the nuclear age. Surely an animal as adaptive and intelligent as the human being can harness its talents for the good, rather than continuing the perverse marriage of technological prowess to the forces of destruction.

That summer on the island I hiked. I watched right whales, gannets and shearwaters. I picked wild raspberries, gooseberries, black- and blueberries, and I made jam. A neighbor brought me a perfect circle of homemade dinner rolls; I traded her some of my jam. Another neighbor built a plywood-and-fiberglass cap for our chimney, saying with confidence, "It will outlast your mom—and maybe you and me." I tried to heal my sense of edginess with long walks on trails to the interior I had never before walked. I picked Labrador tea, meadow rue and sow thistle. I found ponds and bogs I had never seen before, identified birds and plants I had not known, needing to find that no matter what jeopardy the place might face, I had not exhausted the discoveries to be made in what was there. "I went to the woods," wrote Thoreau, "because I wished to live deliberately. . . . I grew in those seasons like corn in the night."

Yet I worried that all I had to offer the wounded world was an account of my experience and the reflections that experience induced. It did not seem enough. One day I sat in the woods beside a blown-down spruce that had lodged in the crotch of a white pine. The standing tree leaned each time the wind gusted, making the blowdown rise up, scrape and creak against the branches that had it pinned. Often I have felt healed by being in the wild. But in this moment, the equation reversed. I suddenly felt that paying attention to one's experience of the world was like sitting by the bedside of a patient during the long hours when one is uncertain whether or not the patient will recover. One is certain only that caring and being present are medicine, whether for healing or merely for dulling the pain. I sat and listened a long time to those abrasions speaking in the unsettling wind.

This is the annual report of my assets at year's end.

chapter 5

In the Territory of Birds

Punta Chueca is a dry and hungry village, a clutter of cement-block houses, ocotillo-rib fences, hairless black dogs and mangy chickens, and a few hundred Seri Indians who have made a more or less permanent encampment on a bleached little crook of sand protruding from the infernal southern reaches of the Sonoran Desert into the Sea of Cortés. Nomadic people accustomed for centuries to moving when water grew scarce, the Seris are pretty new to the idea of staying put. Their parched homeground led them never to camp for more than a month or two in one place. As recently as the 1950s their homes were built of brush and sea turtle bones, their weight on the land slight and brief. But now they have the heavy goods of civilization: cement, electricity, convenience store and satellite dish.

I went there to meet a friend who had been visiting the village for twenty-five years. His friendships among the Seris helped to soften the feeling that my presence there was something hard. He had arranged for us to camp on Isla Tiburón with a local guide and a small group of American students interested in learning how the loss of native language was eroding the Seris' natural history knowledge about indigenous plants and animals. What is this animal's name? Where does it live? What does it use to build its nest? What does it eat? Does it lay eggs? When? How many? What stories do you know about this animal? When is this plant harvested? Is it used for food or medicine? They asked the children in Spanish, the elders in the Seri language. Every animal, some plants, used to have a song. They taught us a few. One about the horned lizard who had gone out to gather firewood, loading it on his back as he climbed into the ironwood tree. Come here, come here, the people in the village called, bring us that firewood. But ants had begun to crawl up his legs and bite him. With all that wood on his back, he could not get them off, lost his balance and fell out of the tree. Every time someone sang this song, the Seris lit up, shaking their heads and muttering with affection, *"Pobrecito, pobrecito."* Poor little one. The lizard, it seemed, carried their burdens, along with his own. He shared humanity with them; they shared animality with the lizard.

A woman told us about a mushroom that looks like a penis, but refused to say more, explaining, "I am a Christian." Then an older woman sang its song. The others laughed so loud we never caught the words, but the woman was too modest to sing it again. She only would say that it was very dirty.

It was in this place that I found myself an accidental tourist in the territory of birds. I did not plan for this to happen, nor did I regret it. We set out across the Infiernillo Channel for Isla Tiburón, five visitors in all, in the care of Ernesto Molino, our Seri guide. He ferried us in his panga over the gray chop to the island's long *bajada,* where we stepped onto twenty stark miles of *cardón,* mesquite and creosote bush with the rosy Sierra Kunkaak rising along the island's spine, its shark-fin summit cutting into the bare sky. We set up our tents and hung a blue plastic tarp over arched ocotillo ribs at an ancient encampment site on the beach. Clamshells and clay shards littered the mealy sand—some thick-walled fragments lipped at the top and some delicate eggshells from the large ollas made for carrying water from the mountain. We found a few discarded metates and manos made of black volcanic stone not native to the place, remnants of a time when eelgrass and mesquite seeds were milled into flour near the place they had been harvested.

Osprey and pelicans dove offshore for fish. A single curlew waded in the shallows, a gull and crow picking their way across the mudflats. Three of our group walked a mile up the beach and found the clean, meatless skeleton of a dolphin stranded above the tide line, its ribs like pairs of stylized doll arms embracing nothing. Three teeth lay bedded in their sockets. We loosened them, stroked the soft ivory, then slipped them in our pockets, one for each of us, to take home as talismans of our good fortune in discovery. It did not matter that our discovery was of death. Being human, we found joy in the new, even if the new was grotesque or played at the timbre of elemental fears. Perhaps with those dead teeth in our pockets we felt we had stolen a little of death's power.

The Seris have lived in the region for over two thousand years, and Isla Tiburón has been significant to them for its clean mountain springs, wild game, and plants gathered for food, medicine, baskets and dyes. They have thirteen names for mesquite, seven of which are for growth stages of the seedpod. The names for eelgrass, another important food plant, signify stages of its life cycle: when it first sprouts, when it grows above the surface of water, when it detaches and floats up, when it piles into windrows on the beach. These are the last hunter-gatherers in Mexico and quite possibly the poorest people in the nation. There were once six groups speaking three dialects scattered around the region. According to Richard Felger, the prominent anthropologist of the culture, the remaining Seris are an amalgamation of survivors from these regions. Their longevity on the west coast of Sonora has been established by carbon dating of eelgrass found in an ancient burial site.

Ernesto wanted to take us to a spring in the mountains, a place where the Seris had gathered water for centuries. We hiked inland toward the crinkled heights, Ernesto marching purposefully through the scrub as if there were a path, his blue satin baseball jacket a beacon ahead while we picked our way, sweaty and leery of rattlesnakes, through the thorns and brush. I guess there was a path in his mind, for he never hesitated unless to explain how the creosote bush provided a decongestant and nerve tonic, the sap of the *torote blanco* served as a cure for cataracts, the roots of ratany were woven into baskets, and blue dye made from ground-up snails mixed with four or five of these plants. One of our group told him that he ought to become a biologist. "I already am a biologist," he answered.

As a community leader, Ernesto had received training in Mexico City in ecotourism. The government hopes that the industry will help to support poor indigenous communities that are less able to live by traditional means because of shrinking and degraded habitats. The Seris have a reputation for being opportunistic. When the Spanish settled in Mexico in the seventeenth century, the nomadic Seris made good use of new resources by raiding and rustling cattle to augment their hunting. In the twentieth century they expanded their subsistence fishing to serve the growing commercial market. But in the Sea of Cortés, as elsewhere, wild resources are strained. There is not much left to fish for, except tourists. Ernesto was not naive about the impact of outsiders. He told us about a rich Mexican who had settled on Seri land and killed off plants by the thousands in order to build his enormous house.

"We got rid of him," Ernesto said, "even though the sky threatened to kill us if we did. We used to fight with guns. Now we fight with knowledge."

He was studying the Mexican Constitution, and though he had his reservations about the negative impact of tourists on Seri land and culture, the options being negligible, he was willing to give it a try.

As we walked farther into the heat of the day, our pace lagged and our eyes wandered to the ground at our feet with more longing than to the heights that still lay an hour ahead. We stopped to rest. Someone found a bleached deer rack. Ernesto said that before the Seris had guns his grandfather had hunted with the whole head of a deer, wearing it on his head, hiding behind a bush, moving gradually closer to the herd. The deer thought the interloper was one of their kind and little by little would approach, until one got so close that the men could jump it. In his lifetime Ernesto had seen one guy do it, and he said that the movements were incredible. "It's dangerous," he cautioned. "If you screw up, the animals are right on top of you."

He said little about other aspects of his grandfather's history, except that the place where we were headed was called "the place where we go when the enemy chases us." We had read about the battles with the Mexican army fought on that ground, the slaughter of women and children who had run to a cave in the mountains to hide. At certain points along the way, Ernesto murmured under his breath, *"Pobrecitos, pobrecitos,"* and we sensed that he knew just what terrible thing had occurred in that spot. Even now the Mexican Marines maintained a small base on the island, though a government decree had designated the place to be under Seri jurisdiction. Some of the people worried that what had happened in Chiapas last year—the official government slaughter of indigenous rebels—might happen here next. I wondered if leading groups of foreigners over ground hallowed by his ancestors' suffering might feel to Ernesto like a sacrilege. I knew that it must be so and also that for the Seris to survive on their homeground, such tours were one of their best bets.

There were six in our party, three men and three women. Perhaps the cause was the heat of high afternoon, perhaps the fact that several of us already had begun to suffer from an unfriendly intestinal colonization, perhaps the sadness and complexity of history had crept into our idle mood, but whatever the cause, after we had stopped in the shade to snack and sip from our canteens, the women decided we were too tired to go on. The men continued up the slope, hoping to reach the mountain spring. We lay in the sparse shade of palo verde and ocotillo to nap and talk about the troubles women save for one another's listening. Mostly it was the subject of men that occupied our conversation, wondering what makes it work or not work between a woman and a man. One told of meeting the man she loves during an outdoor leadership program. After a month in the wilderness they were covered with grime and the stink of their bodies. That's when they fell in love—it was pheromones, she said, I'm sure of it. Another told of her lingering break from a brilliant and charming man who refused during their last year together to touch her. I told of infidelities suffered and the attraction I could not resist for someone new, though I saw in the man the same tendencies that had wounded me before. We lounged in the sweet togetherness of women in which our hopes for love thrive.

While we talked cactus wrens trilled, a gila woodpecker worked the *cardones* and high in the perfect sky a black vulture circled. Lying on our backs, we watched it absently, as we might have watched a small fair-weather cloud, never considering that its presence had anything to do with us. But while the other birds

flitted in and out of our view, the vulture stayed directly over-
head, circling and circling. I began to think it was homing on
some rank thing that lay near us, or on a creature close to dying
that would make a fresh meal. I knew, or thought I knew, that the
presence of a vulture means death.

I do not know what draws such a predator to its table, whether
sight or smell or a synesthetic sense that humans will never
know. The Seris have a story that explains the vulture's skill.
They say that in the beginning of the world the fly invented fire.
They say that now when a fly lands on a dead animal, it makes
fire by rubbing its front legs together and sends smoke signals
telling the vulture where on the desert the carcass lies.

We heard the men coming a long while before they arrived,
men we all loved in friendship, and we knew they would play a
joke on us. The crunch of gravel slowed, then quieted. A set of
antlers rose from behind a bush. We weren't surprised and did
not pretend we were. Still everyone got a good laugh. One guy
asked us if we had seen the vulture circling us. Yes, we answered.
He joked that after camping out we smelled so bad the vulture
thought he might have found something to eat. We all got another good laugh, except Ernesto, who looked sober and shook
his head.

"No, no," he said to the other men, "that's not it at all. The vulture was guarding them, because they are beautiful." We were
puzzled, the gap between our way of seeing and his filling up
with awkward silence. Then he explained that if the men had
gotten lost and not returned, anyone from the village a mile
across the water would have seen the vulture and known where
to find us. It was our turn to look sober, for what was black suddenly looked white, what was harbinger had become protector.

As we started back to camp, the quiet stayed with us, each
holding fast to Ernesto's way of seeing. It was not our way, and

we knew it. That's what made it stick in our imaginations like a puffy airborne seed lodged in thorns. The world looked then both kinder and more dangerous than it had before. We fanned out in search of dead wood for our campfire, hefting bleached gray branches and root burls onto our backs and shoulders.

I migrated to the Atlantic North in the summer to clamber about the bogs and forests I have known since childhood. I was not looking for much, the usual summer pleasures of freedom and peace. But it had become a summer when change impinged upon my sense of refuge. A film crew was headed to our quiet island, the locals hustling to make a buck or gawk at would-be stars who would soon swarm in to produce a celluloid gothic horror story in which molten corpses would crawl from their graves. The spectacle seemed to me nothing to get excited about and so I chose each day to head out as far from the buzz as I could get. And what I found was birds.

Ox Head is a spit of heath overgrown with red-tasseled sorrel, water hemlock (the weed that finished Socrates, not the more familiar and benign coniferous tree) and sheep laurel. The landform does not look at all like an ox. Perhaps oxen once were pastured there and gave the remote promontory its name, as happened with the numerous islets that bear the name Sheep or Ram Island. Ox Head is only a ten-minute walk from Great Pond, where for years I have tempered the impatience induced by muggy July days with floating beneath the spectacle of flocked gulls that turn there in the sky like a daytime zodiac. But I had never set feet to the ground to see what lay beyond my idling nor noticed the promontory's name on an island map I thought I knew by heart. The sheep laurel was the first surprise, its magenta blossoms blaring from the scrub. I have found those bright little parachutes deep in the forest in August, and, knowing the propensity of plants to be specialists, I wondered if it could be the same species blooming in a wild pasture in June. But there was the unmistakable evidence—spokelike anthers rising from the flower's center, bending into pits on the perimeter, a stubborn little generalist not easily deterred from its existence.

Eiders coasted in the shallows, a crisp contrast of white-on-black gliding on the sloppy gray sea. No creatures are better than wild birds at fostering an enchantment with nature, that trance in which history becomes as evanescent as weather and what stays in mind is the perfectly balanced equation of a creature in its place. Birds are radical in their relationship with place, freely ignoring national boundaries, turning urban spaces into forage and nesting grounds, whitewashing entire islands with free-falling excrement, crossing every desert, ocean, mountain and icefield on earth in adapting to seasonal or millennial change. Birds grow, wear, dance and sing their sexual attractions without embarrassment or shame, enact their courtships with high elegance, and mate erotically without remorse. Their flight has inspired both poetry and jet propulsion. In their migration behaviors birds exhibit an intelligence for navigation without instruments far surpassing that of humans, instructing us in the complex geographic relationships a species can accomplish over time.

Birdsong can charm, enrage or terrify. The water music of a hidden Swainson's thrush or canyon wren says that a love of pattern and beauty interweave the creaturely struggle for survival. The merciless nocturnal repetitions of a whippoorwill (John Burroughs recorded 1,088 consecutive choruses of its "purple-RIB" call) is template for an insomniac's theme song. When my mother remembers the whippoorwills that kept us awake at our Connecticut home, she speaks as if they were marauding locusts:

"And every night they came closer and closer to the house." It seemed unnatural that we, in our secure and comfortable home, should be deprived of sleep by creatures we could never see. We hated them. And any student of Edgar Allan Poe can readily conjure the raven's one-word call as the soul-waking messenger of death.

The eiders drifted in the shoals, fitting so well in the place that I could not imagine the evolutionary legacy of strained relationship with climate, food and predators in other places that must have led them to these northern shores. Birds do not do much to change the places they inhabit. If what they need is not there, they move on or die. People make a sorry comparison, finding few places on earth we can live without radically altering them. That is our evolutionary strength, of course, the ability to reshape nature to suit our needs. We have no choice but to transform the surface of the Earth, since we are frail, thin-skinned and vulnerable even to most weather. The average housecat, stranded without provisions in the wild, would stand a better chance of survival than the average civilized human being. But people don't get stranded in the wild today, unless they choose to for adventure, or their plane goes down, or they want to die like an animal. We live in a human-made world of protections and pleasures, drunk on our freedom to move where and when we wish, insulted by any hint of risk we ourselves have not invited, imagining that no condition of nature is so hostile we cannot find a method to gentle it. What we cannot seem to gentle is the hostility inherent in those methods. We make war with nature, nations and ourselves in order to be at peace.

Elie Wiesel, speaking of the Nazi Holocaust, has said that winds of madness blow through history, times when blindness prevails and people become too morally sick to save others from suffering, humiliation and death. He refers to employees of the regime who worked in the death camps, unable to see the evil in what they were doing. The human relationship with nature often looks like a form of madness which, taken to its megalomaniacal extreme, imagines we can live in an entirely human-made world—the ultimate civilization in space—as if we had no material or spiritual need for the other species on Earth, as if we had no obligation to protect them from suffering, humiliation and death, as we would protect our own.

This madness is embedded in the language historically used to describe the moral enemies of civilization: "heathen," "pagan" and "savage." Pulled up at their roots, the words are emblems of the nature-as-clay-for-our-hands view. "Heathen," descended from the Old English version of "heath," meaning "open uncultivated ground covered by heather or related plants," once was a timid descriptor meaning simply "inhabiting open country." "Pagan" derives from the Latin *pagus,* referring to a rural district or village; "savage" from the Latin word for forest, *silva.* The fact that all three words once described people who lived more rustically than urban dwellers and then came to signify idolaters is an artifact of a long historical period in which threats to civilization lay primarily outside of its urban centers. Those threats included the elements, predatory animals and foreign invaders who were not "civilized," that is, not subject to *our* laws. From these dangers—the lawlessness of the wild—our ancestors found protection within the fortress, physical and moral, of the city, and these three words became their shields.

But the world is smaller now, and civilization is its own worst enemy. The barbarians have nearly all been murdered, a process that began three thousand years ago and will end in our lifetimes as the last of the original forms of humanity turn into capitalists. Everywhere on the planet a radical hybridization of cultures—of nationality and ethnicity, of rural and urban people, of tribal and corporate and even genetic structures—is taking place, and it is all held together by invisible electronic threads that beam up from our homes and offices to transmitters we have sent into orbit around the Earth. We do not have a language to describe this dizzying turn of the cultural axis, for as soon as we find a name it becomes obsolete. Once it seemed an impossible task to draw the curved face of Earth on a flat map. The new map of the world is too complex to imagine, for it must represent not only major landforms, bodies of water and human habitation, but also the whizzing transcultural movement of our marketing, entertainment and communication technologies, and the brown air they leave in their wakes; not only the nationalities and ethnicities, but also habitats, natural resources, extinctions and preserves. We have so many ways to view the world we can hardly stand to look at it. And if we would be honest and honorable to Earth's history as the metastory to human history, we would need to draw a map of the losses witnessed since our species arrived on the scene, to keep alive at least a mental presence of the Hun and Taino, the Pict and Pericue; and of the birds, which have paid for human wealth more dearly than any others—the long-lost dodo, passenger pigeon, dusky seaside sparrow, New Zealand laughing owl, Jamaican macaw, Samoan wood rail, Guadalupe flicker, the Ryuku kingfisher, the Lord Howe Island white-eye, the Hawaiian honeycreeper, koa-finch, akialoa, kakawahie and ou.

Aldo Leopold proposed "the land ethic" as a possible and necessary new element in an expanding sense of human ethics. "Our first ethics," he wrote, "dealt with the relation between individuals. . . . Later accretions dealt with relations between the individual and society." Roderick Nash in *The Rights of Nature* has expanded the territory, tracking how the extension of ethics to the natural world has begun to take hold. "One of the most

remarkable ideas of our time," he writes, "[is] the belief that ethical standing does not begin and end with human beings."

> *The emergence of this idea that the human-nature rela-*
> *tionship should be treated as a moral issue conditioned*
> *and restrained by ethics is one of the most extraordinary*
> *developments in recent intellectual history. Some believe it*
> *holds the potential for fundamental and far-reaching*
> *change in both thought and behavior comparable to that*
> *which the ideal of human rights and justice held at the*
> *time of the democratic revolutions in the seventeenth and*
> *eighteenth centuries.*

Most recent studies of biodiversity assume that between 50
and 90 percent of the world's current plant and animal species
will disappear within the next hundred years as a result of
human impact. According to biologist E. O. Wilson we are in
the midst of one of the great extinction spasms of geologic history. Even using the most cautious parameters, he estimates that
the number of species doomed each year is twenty-seven thousand; each day is seventy-four, and each hour is three. Birds are
among the most vulnerable, the canaries in the coal mine that
are first to show the signs of danger. Within the past four centuries, 171 species and subspecies of bird have gone extinct. The
more we learn about this hemorrhaging of life from the planet,
the sicker we feel. When we watch a flock of birds pass by, we see
our own wild innocence recede.

I left the eiders to pick my way along the shore, the fog closing in, chilling my bare arms and making me eager for home.
Along the intertidal stones of low tide the salt grass glistened
even in the fog's dulled light. Ahead a sudden flurry broke out,
squawking balls of fuzz scattering in all directions to get out of

my path. The mother—a mallard or black duck, dusky body and morpho blue wing patches—limped away with wings drooped, staggering, dragging her right wing on the ground. According to her plan, I stared, held still, then followed, wondering if she was really wounded. I had read about broken-wing display as an avian defense of the young, but I never had witnessed it. The strategy would not have done a bit of good if I had meant business with buckshot. Such a defense was invented for less successful predators than the aggressors of our species, but against a merely curious interloper it worked.

I forgot the ducklings, which must have reached deep cover in the scrub. I was fixed on the mother's deception as she scuttled low over the rocks, flapping pathetically along the sand, leading me farther and farther on. I was still not convinced that she was faking until, far down the beach with a final glance in my direction, she hobbled into the water, floated a moment, rearranged her wings, and lifted with perfect ease to return to the nest.

There is not a single day of any year when I do not see or hear a bird, though I do not always notice that I am seeing and hearing them. But never before had birds insisted themselves upon me so emphatically. A few days later, feeling cramped in the house, I headed for the island's wooded backside. Not much there except beech trees, balsam and hemlock, a trail hugging the edge of a cliff that drops hundreds of feet to the sea. One naturally formed breakwater holds a sheltered lagoon, where salmon pens float attached to a floating walkway and the red shack of the man who tends the smolts until ready for market. I have always wanted to ask him to run me out there in his dory and show me around. But more appealing than learning about the island's shaky industrial future is exploring its sylvan past, as if to walk far enough into the unpeopled woods were to find one's deeper origin.

I followed the scrappy trail along basalt cliffs, stopping at a lookout point to watch the work of fishermen a quarter mile to the north. A row of dories had been hauled up on the stone beach; one was puttering out to the salmon pens, but was so distant I could not hear its motor, only saw the bow rise as the throttle opened then settle back down as it closed. Whatever work was going on looked easy, something one man in one small boat could manage. I continued on far from anyone's work, the breeze rising from time to time, stirring tree scent into the air, acrid leaf mold and sweet gummy balsam. The fragrance spun up in gusts and eddies. Spruces near the cliff had been stunted by the wind, grown bare on the leeward side that winter had abused. The green sea far below had no sound, yet was so clear white stones were visible beneath the slough and heave. Miles across the channel lay a village, a distant speckle of buildings, small and quaint, folded into the lumpy blue mass of the land. It looked harmless posed against the broad scale of sea and land and sky. Somewhere underlying the intervening channel lay the imaginary line that separates Canada from the United States, a friendly border compared to most, one I have crossed yearly, almost as freely as a bird, in order to feed on these woods.

I walked farther than I ever had before into the tannin musk, into bunchberries littering the ground like white confetti thrown everywhere, into the apple green ferns, young, not yet filling the understory with the shoulder-high meadows they would become by midsummer. The deeper in I got the more I gloated about my luck to know such a place—no tacky resort, no spandex high-tech wilderness jocks, no Saturday horde, no products and profits and hype. Just woods, piped with thrush and sparrow song and wind. Maybe it is a sorry state of affairs to have to leave human culture, if only for a day, in order to see the world go luminous again with significance, but so be it. In this place I can walk the misanthropy out of my system, the rancor at what people have ruined with their greed and blindness, the fear that I will lose my love and wonder for the world.

A rough sapling bridge crossed a stream at a place deerhunters and snowmobilers use in fall and winter. In summer the logs grow mossy from lack of traffic. Those miles and hours of woods seem to own themselves, though I have heard that a wealthy Scandinavian has bought most of this land on speculation. People used to call it "the Queen's land," more out of respect for British royalty than for fact. The island was settled by runaway Loyalists who opposed the American Revolution. I do not care who owns it as long as I am free to wander there.

I was heading down into a sheltered draw, the trail overarched with dappled beech leaves, when a shriek shot out of the green. It sounded like a gull, though sharper and strong, one note repeated and repeated, "kaak," "kaak," "kaak." I saw nothing but trees. Then a gray mass erupted from the foliage, diving low and fast straight for my face, big as an eagle. Its eyes were bullets aiming for mine. I dropped to my knees, wrapping my arms over my head. The muscular gust of it Doppler-shifted over me. Then the woods went silent, though I could hear the creature's eyes on my back. Slowly I unfolded from my crouch, turned to see the bird perched and glaring on a high limb at the opposite end of the draw.

I watched it. It watched me. I spoke softly, though I do not know where the hope came from that my words might convince it of anything. It let me stand. For a moment.

Then came the shrill kaaking call and the warrior decked me again. My courage was up, since I had survived the first kamikaze dive, so this time I tried to spot field marks—not an easy task when one is wondering just how close the lovely hooked beak

and metal-sharp talons are going to come to one's eyes. I picked
out some detail—soft gray plumage on the back, white breast
with delicate tweedy bars. Black eye stripes, perhaps, though
from this vantage I did not see much of a profile. Its face looked
strangely owl-like. After knocking me to my knees three times,
it figured I had been sufficiently humbled and let me pass,
though, just in case, I twirled my walking stick over my head in
order to make myself a more complicated target. The bird's eyes
burned on my back.

Hours later on my return, I had no choice but to take the
same path home. The woods had grown tame by then, water
music of the little birds bubbling up and sunlight dappling my
arms. I wondered if I would recognize the place where the encounter had occurred, then wondered how the bird might be
reading me as I got close. Big, noisy, smelly animal with clothes
and stick. But a brain, even a bird or animal one, is not a machine. It reads not isolated sensory facts, but the gestalt, the integrated totality, of a situation. Something of my thoughts and
emotions must be attainable to any creature I encounter, some
response both learned and immediate to the complexity that I
am. This is why the common wisdom about dogs is that they can
smell a person's fear, or about street punks that you must not
look them in the eye. This is why my housecats slink away from
me when they have misbehaved and I catch them in the act. Just
the aura of my scowl sends them running.

So what had been my gestalt at the time of the raptor's attack?
I confess it, I had been gloating, spilling my joy all over the
woods as if I owned them; haughty, feeling safe that there was no
creature here—rattlesnake, grizzly or cougar—that could harm
me. Though I enjoyed the feeling of a risk-free wilderness, that
view was not shared in the eyes that peered from trees and scrub.
To them (in whatever manner they were capable of perceiving

this—not as *idea,* surely, but as the bodily knowledge of startle or flinch) I was the dominant predator for miles around, not a quality that would draw creatures to my side. I began to feel the possibility of a more emphatic greeting from the fledged guardian of that darkened draw, and so as I got close to the place I wrapped my sweater around my neck for armor and raised my walking stick for a scepter.

I am thoroughly a product of Western culture and happily so. I was raised in a house where classical music and Shakespearean plays spun on the family turntable. I studied the piano and flute, took modern dance classes and secreted myself in the delicious privacy of my room to take Dostoevsky, Anne Frank and Charles Dickens to bed with me. I read books as if I were possessed by them, my spirit occupied by their realities in a way that satisfied my hunger more than did the actualities of daily life. I learned very young to love the best of the human world, those creations that bring the inner world to light. But learning how to communicate with wild animals is not generally a component of even the best North American education. When we talk to animals, it is usually to our pets, whom we address in baby talk or commands. In earlier forms of human culture, people spoke to animals as if they were elders, prayed to them, asked for their guidance, forbearance and forgiveness, read their behavior as we would a fine book. Animals played a significant role in people's inner world, as well as the outer one, and a kind of communication with them, such as Ernesto's reading of the black vulture in Seriland, was possible.

And so as I strode into the draw with my scepter in hand, feeling powerless and foolish and scared, I spoke to the memory of my attacker.

"Please forgive me for trespassing on your land. I am small and harmless, and I will soon be gone."

But there was no sign of the creature. Perhaps it was lodged deep in the foliage looking down in disdain. Perhaps it had gone off on a hunt. The beech trees at either end of the draw where it had earlier perched stood out among the others, having been dignified by the bird's presence. I was awake to the place as it might be when no humans are there, eager to pass through and let it be so.

Since birds kept insisting themselves upon me, I decided to take the upper hand and seek them out. I signed on to a charter leaving our island and heading for the bird island that lies a few hours to the south. Machias Seal Island is a fifteen-acre outcropping of granite and weeds a dozen miles from much of anything but ocean. Once feared by fogbound mariners of the North Atlantic, the hazardous area has been marked since 1832 with a light station maintained by the Canadian government. It became a sanctuary for nesting seabirds in 1944. A small team of technicians and researchers, along with the ceaseless din of their diesel-powered generator, live at the refuge. Most of the acreage is a tumble of boulders and rocky shore. The higher ground is covered with a lush green meadow, the consequence of birds, people and domestic animals, all of whom have added to the seed lore of the island. Sedges, grasses, asters, parsley docks and herbs have taken hold. And for a few months of the year Seal Island, as it is familiarly known to the locals, is populated by thousands of migrating birds.

"Last year I didn't know the difference between a puffin and a penguin," joked our guide, as we bobbed out past tubular plastic salmon pens in a fishing boat refitted with benches and canvas canopy for tourists. He was new to the job, but so is nearly everyone in a region where the beast of ecotourism is just beginning to wake. Still, he ably pointed out the common murres, gannets, black guillemots and eiders we encountered riding the swells that rose and fell around us like breathing flesh. We crossed MacGregor's Shoals, a rough upwelling, then beyond to where the water flattened into a greasy sheen. We passed a raft of sea ducks, then a scattering of storm petrels that flitted and dipped low over the water like swallows.

"They're named after Saint Peter," the guide reported, "because they can walk on water just like he did." I was not sure about the accuracy of either the Biblical or natural history, but I was glad to know the name of the small, dark travelers.

As we neared Seal Island, a few scattered puffins and razorbills floated by. Pelagic birds, they spend their lives far at sea, except during a few months of breeding and nurture when they nest on remote patches of land.

"And we think we have hard lives," quipped our guide like a stand-up comic. Like most places serving as sanctuaries for wild animals, Seal Island is increasingly a mecca for naturalists, bird-watchers and photographers. As we approached the little bump on the horizon, we saw two tour boats already at anchor offshore. Our boatload joined the party, the dozen of us riding a dory in batches of four across the coastal chop to the rockweed-draped shore, our skipper standing astern at the tiller doing his own version of Saint Peter. Running down from the island's summit—all of fifty feet above sea level—the rusted tracks of an old tramway traversed a stained and eroded concrete ramp. The wildlife warden greeted us from the ramp. A ten-foot-wide chasm separated us, waves slurring over rocks far enough below to make us check our footing. He hefted a two-by-ten plank across the gorge, and we single-filed from the slippery rocks over a churning inlet to the battered concrete on shore.

The warden's Wildlife Service cap and jacket were streaked

and smeared with the whitewash of his charges. While he stood at plank's end to help the new arrivals, he told those who had crossed to go the end of the ramp, pick up a stake we would find there and wait. We followed the instructions, bemused but obedient, while the others teetered and joked about walking the plank. Herring stakes—three feet long and a half inch square—have been used for the last century to string fish through the gills for hanging in the smokehouses. The islands in the region once prospered making smoked herring, but they now run only a few small operations. Most herring is shipped to the mainland, where it is factory-processed with "artificial smoke flavoring." The old blackened stakes turn up everywhere—excellent for building a pea fence or staking tomatoes, and, I was about to learn, for deflecting the assaults of hyperactive Arctic terns.

The air over Seal Island stormed with birds. They swarmed, dove and curved in aerobatic flourishes, their tweaking calls fierce and shrill. Some flew past us with silver fry in their red bills heading for nests in the grass. Others aimed their needle-nosed beaks at the tops of our heads and dove. When we had all assembled, the warden led us on, a little parade of marchers with fish-stake batons held over our heads, dozens of terns slamming toward us and screaming, cutting their dives just short of the tops of our stakes.

We gathered on the deck beside the lightkeeper's house for orientation. Regulations strictly controlled the nature of our visit—walk slowly, only on paths, do not linger in any place, give a wide berth to orange flags marking nests. We may stay on the island for three hours. We may cross the grass to the far shore where puffins and razorbills nest only on our way to and from a blind. We may remain in a blind for twenty-five minutes. Four people are allowed in the blind at one time. We must move quickly when we enter. The longer we are visible the farther away from their young the parents will fly.

Some twenty-four hundred pairs of arctic terns nest on Seal Island (numbers may have been as high as thirty-five hundred pairs in the 1940s), along with two hundred pairs of common terns, and a few roseates. In addition, about eleven hundred pairs of puffins, three hundred pairs of razorbilled auks and fifty pairs each of common eiders and Leach's storm petrels nest on Seal Island. All of these seabirds come here for one reason, to breed, and they have established a community in which each species succeeds in that mission, each gaining some advantage from the presence of the others, or at least each finding no quarrel with another species so important as to upset the balance they have together established.

Most numerous are the arctic terns, which arrive at the end of May, laying their eggs in exposed nests, barely more than a matted area on top of the grass. Chicks hatch in late June, two to a nest, and need constant protection from preying gulls. Terns attack any potential enemy by diving toward it and letting out a rapid series of shrieks. The dive usually stops short of its target, but a solid strike is not unusual. I found this out when, wondering if our fish-stake defense was really necessary, I lowered my guard and learned in an instant the sharp insult of beak against scalp. By the end of July the young are on the wing above the island, practicing for long-distance flight. Juveniles and adults depart together in August to join other arctic terns that have nested in Iceland, Greenland and other northern refuges. Their migration route is the most ambitious on Earth. They will fly across the North Atlantic, pass along the west coast of Europe and Africa, then southward to their winter home in the Antarctic Ocean. They will reach and likely circle the Antarctic ice pack, an annual migration pattern of twenty-five to thirty thousand miles, a distance greater than a trip around the world. Each year they will return to the north to breed, living and repeating this global dance for as long as twenty-five years.

In spite of the phenomenal migratory talent of the arctic tern, it is the puffin that draws most human visitors to Seal Island. A stout bird with a broad bill, emphatically banded with red and yellow, the Atlantic puffin is the bird of choice in this region for images on mugs, T-shirts and posters. It is the creature that makes this place unique, stirring up immediate human affection with its attractive oddness and the apparently sad-eyed look of its facial markings. Nesting in sheltered burrows among the boulders, the puffin does not need such an aggressive defense policy as the tern. It tends to pose cooperatively for photographers, gawking at humans as curiously as humans gawk at it.

When my turn came to observe from the blind, I was lucky to wind up with a man leading a group of birdwatchers from Massachusetts. He, along with two of his charges and an excellent spotting scope, was already stationed in the darkened compartment, a few foot-tall plywood portals opened to the avian spectacle. The man was speaking in a hushed tone as I slipped into the blind and jockeyed past his tripod and students to take the last available window at the far wall. There was a beautifully human tenderness to their voices as each in turn took the scope and acquiesced to the newly seen. Watching the melee of birds that freckled the air, water and rocks, they focused on the sulfur-yellow flesh lining the mouth of a razorbill in breeding plumage. The bird kept its distance, standoffish, unlike the puffins that perched on the boulders closest to the blind and watched us watching them through our portals. The birdman told us that the puffins are calm birds. Even after their chicks hatch, they show little aggression unless one goes into another's burrow.

Cooperatively, one touched down on the nearest boulder with three fresh sardines drooping from its bill, stood idling before us to be photographed, then hopped between the rocks to deliver its catch. In addition to concealing the nests, the boulders serve as launching points. A puffin's small pointed wings are good for paddling underwater, but they make getting aloft a challenge.

The center of the puffin world is Iceland, where there may be as many as ten million of the birds. Seal Island, located at the lower end of the Bay of Fundy, is one of the most southerly colonies in their breeding range. Most successful mating takes place at sea, and according to one researcher "a hoarse cry at the moment of pairing has been reported." Noisy billing is a part of courtship, one bird nuzzling and nibbling the other's bill, until they start repeatedly knocking their bills together broadside, other puffins rushing over to observe the displaying pair. The peak of the hatch is in mid-June. For a month or more both parents deliver small fish to the young. At the end of July they desert them for up to a week, during which time the juveniles learn to find their way from their burrows to the ocean surrounding the island. By August the adults and young depart for the open sea.

Because they are so placid, puffins suffer heavy predation by black-backed gulls. Their only other significant predator is people, who in the 1800s persecuted the birds for eggs, meat, feathers and pure mean fun, wiping out the populations on some breeding islands. Black-backed gulls, which often breed in puffin colonies, will work in pairs to catch a puffin in flight and pull the living bird to pieces. After the kill they will eat the entrails and breast muscles, turn the skin inside out like a glove, pick the bones and skull clean. Sometimes a gull will swallow the head whole and regurgitate the undigestable parts. Gulls steal fish from puffins, eat their eggs and young.

Some of this behavior represents genetic learning and some

bird culture—what's learned through fledgling experience and by watching conspecifics. Genetic learning is not fast, but by definition it has stood the test of time. How long did it take for puffins to learn that by nesting near terns they could remain pacifists and benefit from the aggressive defense tactics of their neighbors? How long did it take for terns to learn that by nesting near more vulnerable neighbors they could improve the odds for their own offspring? The breeding community on Seal Island has been shaped by each species's drive for survival. In some instances the drive is expressed as survival of the fittest, in some survival of the most cooperative.

Earth is a giant laboratory of learning, every living thing doing what it can to make its life work and meet the demands of changing circumstances. Some creatures depend mostly on the long-learning of their genetic history. The oldest bird, *Archaeopteryx*, lived 140 million years ago. Six fossil specimens of it have been found in Bavarian limestone. This Jurassic early bird is no longer around, but some of its contemporaries are—frogs, squid, lobsters. Human beings are Quaternary latecomers—only one hundred thousand years old, unless one stretches the definition to claim our history begins one million years ago with the Pleistocene hominids. Even so, if duration of time on Earth were the measure of species worth, we would be pretty poor currency. Of course, we have made up for lost time with our impressive capacities for creating cultures and languages. These relatively fast methods of learning may be different from those of other species, but they are no better. The trouble for the other species is that we are moving so fast that they, stuck with their poky genes, cannot catch up.

The Massachusetts birdman nudged me over to the scope, pointing out the refinement of the thin white line running along the razorbill's covert, the sheen of its tuxedo black body. Two razorbills began courting, the male clicking his bill against the female's, then mounting her, flapping to stay aloft, then both staggering into a crevice to their nest. More razorbills than puffins seemed to be standing around in pairs, and I wondered how the two species differ in pair-bonding habits. I wondered too what the idea of an individual means to species for which life is so collective.

The birdman was eager and knowledgeable, and he brightened when he saw me taking notes, leaned close to whisper and guide me into what he knew. I could not keep up the pace. A few land birds showed up, savannah sparrow and—was that tree swallow or barn swallow? That growling sound like a chain saw starting in the distance—was that the razorbill or puffin? The black bird with white eye ring—a murre or an auk? My head swam, but I no longer cared about the information. It was the hushed excitement of a man aroused by nature's complexity that owned me. I asked if he knew about the local raptors—yes, a bit—and I told him about how I had been strafed in the woods.

"Had to have been a goshawk. They can look pretty big when they're coming right at you."

I learned that goshawks live on forest edges near cliffs and swamps, where they have ample flight corridors for hunting. They hunt squirrels, grouse and rabbits either in fast searching flights or by the perch-and-wait technique. In an all-out chase, a goshawk will plunge through heavy cover in reckless pursuit for nearly a mile; its speed on impact can be fifty miles an hour. During breeding season it goes to great lengths to communicate its territorial prerogatives.

When our group of four left the blind and returned to the others waiting on the lightkeeper's deck, the birdman reported gleefully to his pals, "This lady got decked by a goshawk!" And we all felt wonderful that such a thing was possible.

. . .

Back home I fell into a two-hour nap, bobbing in and out of sleep, feeling the swells of the sea and seeing stout puffins, watchful, gliding by. My rest was so fitful I was uncertain if I was asleep or awake, until I saw puffins floating by in the air beside my bed and knew I was in a dream of their presence that made me feel awake.

I travel for the reasons people always have traveled—Delphi, Lourdes, Grand Tour, Walkabout or Disneyland. I travel because a hunger leads me from place to place, a hunger that tells me I can be replenished by the world. It is something the birds have known all along, this knowledge making my head swim that the world in all its complexity is something we are born to devour, moving from place to place to satisfy the need that keeps us alive as long as it refuses to quit.

Once in the desert I watched a pair of Harris's hawks, magnificent in their chocolate and chestnut plumage, nurturing their young in the notch of a many-pronged saguaro. Two chicks perched and waited in the bramble of desiccated sticks and weeds that had been packed into a nest. They were too young to fly, scraggly in their adolescent plumage, mottled, awkward on long legs ruffled like Victorian pantaloons. At midday the parents stood panting, tongues pumping against the drying sun. At dusk they departed to hunt, and in the cool fading light the chicks pulled idly on strings of bloody flesh. Then they lay down, preened and rearranged themselves on the nest. It seemed peaceful, this family life of killing, eating and growing up. Sunset flared across the western sky turning the mountains red, the facing clouds in the east infected with that rosy light. All the voices of the desert birds grew active, flocking and calling in their last errands of the day.

chapter 6

Beyond the Brown Border

*TEPOZTLÁN, MEXICO—One simmering Sunday in May, a
hundred peasant farmers stormed a luxurious hillside man-
sion, and, in a scene out of an old newsreel of the 1910 Revolution, pounded on the gates with machetes and their
clenched fists until the wealthy owners abandoned their
brunch and fled.*

—New York Times, July 1996

On the flight to Mexico City I started reading Octavio Paz's *The
Labyrinth of Solitude.* I had started it several times before, but
never persevered. This time, I thought, the odds were better. I
was heading for an extended stay in Oaxaca, and I carried with
me questions about the Mexican culture. How well could a person from a rich nation—the richest—know one of the poorest?
What did Mexico have to do with me as an American? I could
speak only restaurant Spanish. And my ignorance of Mexican
culture felt like a burden, considering that I had lived next door
to the nation for seven years, and my home city of Tucson was
something of a cultural annex to its southern neighbor. Over
those years I had assembled a bleak collage of the place: a nation
troubled by drug dealing, official corruption, whimsical vio-

lence, desperate economics and near ecological collapse. I knew that millions of people born in Mexico live in the United States, and that they bring with them family and personal affiliations that, out of economic and emotional necessity, violate the international border. I knew that Mexico was a place Americans go to score drugs and cheap sex, to binge on booze and fall into stupid oblivion, or to live out a last shot at the mythical Wild West, riding horseback into the past and brawling one's way back out. Perhaps because I have crossed the Canadian border every summer as free and benign as a bird, I found it difficult to accept that the Mexican border had become such a volatile and violent place. Gloria Anzaldua calls it "an open wound" where the first and third worlds meet and bleed.

Once when driving in eastern Arizona near the border, I had seen three Mexican youths wearing camouflage pants and tank tops, one carrying a small canvas rucksack, all the luggage any of them had, bolt across the Interstate in front of my car, looking back over their shoulders then ahead, back and forth, back and forth, with electric intensity. They were heading from south to north, and I knew they were running for their lives. I knew this was an act repeated hundreds, maybe thousands, of times each day—that poor Mexicans died of thirst in the desert, drowned in the Rio Grande, suffocated in sealed trucks, railroad cars and drainage pipes, looking for safe passage out of their poverty. I knew that since the 1994 peso crash, even doctors had left home to pick up fishing nets and fruit crates in the United States, and I knew that what I might spend on a fancy cup of coffee and a muffin would equal the daily wage of the fortunate Mexican who stayed at home and had a job.

What I knew were aspects of Mexico's public face, as seen from the North, but I did not know a thing about the quality and complexity of daily life in Mexico. Paz writes that "the historical memory of Americans is European, not American." I was traveling to change that in myself, not just to encounter the American other, but to see myself as that other. I felt foreign already, aloft with a planeload of brown-faced travelers who knew where they were going, while I had no idea what to expect.

According to news reports of the Tepoztlán uprising, the extremes between rich and poor in Mexico are among the worst in the world. In the year or so following the devaluation of the peso, the number of Mexicans living in extreme poverty rose from five million to twenty-two million; seventeen thousand local companies folded; in Mexico City the number of children who lived and worked in the streets doubled, while in a swanky neighborhood a second Gucci boutique opened.

"The only thing that one can feel is embittered," said Guillermo Noriega Garcia, a fifty-six-year-old farmer who took part in the assault on the twenty-acre estate that stood in the middle of parched subsistence farms. "How can it be that one man has everything and others don't even have water?"

It is an old story. In the 1580s Michel de Montaigne wrote that Brazilian Indians, who had been brought to Europe as specimens of the cannibal world, were upset by the injustices they witnessed in civilized society:

> . . . they had noticed that there were among us men full and gorged with all sorts of good things, and that their other halves were beggars at their doors, emaciated with hunger and poverty; and they thought it strange that these needy halves could endure such an injustice and did not take the others by the throat, or set fire to their houses.

Such is the Mexico that resort tourists do not want to see— the poverty, disease, bitterness and violence born of inequity.

I wanted not to fear that inequity, not to fear for myself because of my relative wealth. This is the Mexico that shadows our national prosperity, the Mexico that carries our wealth like cement sacks on its back. This is the Mexico I could not decipher from the North. All I knew was that I hungered for difference, for a culture held together by something other than corporate logos and TV shows, by something that had sprung from American soil before Europeans arrived to hybridize and sell it.

A year earlier on my first trip to the state of Michoacán, I had visited the ruins at San Felipe los Alzati, a small site from the Aztec period that had been partially restored after a local farmer discovered it in the 1970s and asked the government to protect it. Now, because the government was broke, the preservation work had stopped. A stepped face of cobbled rock rose in a pyramid from rubble and weeds to overlook the tilled patchwork valley below. Pottery shards and obsidian chips littered the ground.

The guide, a young Mexican wearing a mesh polyester baseball cap, explained that we were standing at a ceremonial center and astronomical observatory. There had been a ball court and, below, the marketplace. His account of the history was a confused rendering of conflict and succession between tribes and mercenaries contemporary with the Aztecs. While he talked, from time to time he ground a scorpion under his boot or leaned to pick up a shard, handing it to one of our group. He led us to a rock quarry, weedy stones piled in a jumble, some cut with stelae of snail, rattlesnake, deer and spiral. He told us to step only on top of the stones. *Serpientes,* he cautioned, poking a stick into dark crevices to let the snakes know we were coming. One flat stone the size of a file folder bore the carved image of a scorpion, and when he tilted the stone up to show us the carving an actual scorpion woke from its cool bed to squirm in the light.

The guide kept talking, his eyes on us until he had seen that we had seen it, then he dug it into the earth with his heel. He picked up another rock, pointing out the chip marks made with a harder stone.

"The spiral," he said, "stands for the cycle of birth and death—a symbol of these people. When someone was born, a leader would start an engraving on a stone, beginning at the center, then continuing for that person's whole life. Here's a short one—this person must have died young."

That spiral came back to me as I flew south. There I was, setting out from the small point of my origin, circling out into widening circles, trying to take in more and more of the world, trying to make clear the edge of my awareness, without losing the centripetal force of the center that holds the spiral together.

I changed planes in Mexico City, having descended into the stained, industrial air that announces the highest density of human population in the world. An ethnobotanist once told me that thirty miles from that pall indigenous communities of a few thousand people still live relying entirely on native crops, but it seemed unimaginable that the city's allure had not drawn them away from the land. It seemed unimaginable, too, that one could feel at ease in an airport where gun-toting officials were as routine as porters: here three policemen purposefully gripping automatic rifles slung over their shoulders; here two teenage *federales* chatting idly, one twirling his weapon on his forearm, as if doodling in the air with a giant pen. No one seemed bothered by their presence, everyone bustling to get luggage, exchange currency or meet a flight; but the firearms spoke volumes about the tension and volatility underlying business-as-usual in Mexico.

I have flown some clunker airlines south of the border. Once, on a flight from La Paz in a vintage DC-9 that felt like an airborne dump truck, the Spanish-speaking crew, as we started to level, popped in the wrong English-language cassette, and the few gringos on board felt the jumpstart of listening to the crash tape—"Remove your glasses and jewelry," "Brace yourself either by . . ."—as we banked gently over the turquoise sea, the pristine desert flanks of Isla del Espíritu Santo below.

But the Mexicana plane from Mexico City to Oaxaca was a slick new F100 jet, the flight attendants dressed in international corporate style—navy trousers, blazers, crisp white shirts—the rituals and instructions for takeoff identical to what I would hear at home, and I thought with nationalistic pride, *We* invented air travel, this way of living that now the world wants, this velocity and fashion that unite the world's differences. A Muzak version of "If You're Going to San Francisco" wafted on the plane's manufactured air; dark-skinned passengers wore Guess jeans, Flintstones T-shirts and urban-gelled, Indian-black hair, the styles of our culture having bled south of the border, if not the substance. Or perhaps style *is* our primary substance, what we export, what the rich *and* poor of the world want even more than they want our democratic structure of government. Capitalism has succeeded in creating a global culture where all ideology has failed. The cloth of our national fabric is not the American flag, but blue denim Levi's, a style boasting that once we had to work the land, but now we can wear the workman's clothes without getting them dirty.

I woke after a tossing night of goat sounds, barking dogs and fireworks in the streets, to the rocky sound of a cart wheeling over the cobblestones below my window. The goat bleated on, crying for attention the world would never give. Parrots whistled and cooed in the hotel courtyard. And slowly human voices began to marble the morning air. Across the street, past jumbled mission-tile and sheet-metal roofs, a family pushed a wooden cart out of their yard and down the block to the intersection of two side streets, where they unfolded a portable restaurant, set out three tall wooden stools and began dishing out soup. The conversation between cook and customer was gentle and familiar, carrying up to my window like the scent of a wild, sweet herb.

My breakfast was a happily chaotic family affair, children serving the handful of guests at a large common table while caged parrots in the courtyard argued and three or four generations of the proprietor's family drifted through the courtyard cooing back at the birds, giving directions to a disoriented tourist, cooking eggs and beans in the cluttered kitchen open to view through a window beside the dining table, murmuring and laughing in conversation with one another. The meal was long and slow, paced by the telling of travelers' stories. A couple from London had arrived after days in the air and in airports to find they had no hotel reservations. They sat rumpled and grateful at our table while the proprietor telephoned around town for a room. Two graduate students from New York had taken a bus from Mexico City to Oaxaca. It had broken down, and they had been stuck sweltering for hours in the middle of nowhere. They had read books and listened to fragments of conversation, happy for the inconvenience that let them in on local small talk. One passenger, a woman full of loud complaint, thought they could not understand Spanish and said, "Oh, sure, the Americans are happy. They're always happy. They have plenty of money." It made the Americans even happier to see how they were being seen, even if the portrait was not flattering.

It was Saturday and the guests who had been in town for a while told about visiting the market at the Central de Abastos. I

had not come to Mexico for shopping and wondered what the
fuss was about, but so bright was the glow of their enthusiasm
that I decided to take their advice.

Oaxaca, I soon learned, is a walking city. You can get from
anywhere to anywhere in half an hour or so. And along the way
you will pass things you will want not to have missed: colonial
cathedrals built of cool green stone; a woman passing by on her
errands who stops to cross herself, kissing the hand as it blesses
and speaking the words softly aloud for protection or guidance
or succor; vendors of amber pendants, or little sacks of sliced papaya and pineapple, or tiny pamphlets containing "Immortal
Phrases"; a chocolate mill with a wall open to the street, cacao
beans, cinnamon bark and sugar funneled into the grinder,
stirred with a wooden paddle until transformed into grainy
brown ooze that perfumes the air; the buzz of doorbells as the
tortilla vendor makes her morning rounds house to house; the
drab exterior of a walled house suddenly breaking as a gate
opens onto a cobbled courtyard graced with cascading
bougainvillea; the music of water vendors pedaling their carts
along cobbles and singing out, *"El agua, el agua."*

Had I followed the pamphlet advice for a woman traveling
solo—don't walk alone at night, never get into a cab alone, never
look attractive, don't carry more luggage than you can carry on
the run—I would have seen nothing. Only once in several weeks
of walking the city was I threatened by a man. He hustled up
from behind me, whispering words in my ear, the meaning of
which I could not understand, though the intent was clear and
dangerous. I tightened and hurried down the block to where the
crowd was thick. By then the man was gone. Among the travelers' stories I had heard were plenty to make me nervous. A
woman had been bitten by a dog, apparently a stray, one of the
city's numerous scurvied street dogs. She feared it was rabid.

Few Mexican dogs know the privilege of veterinarian care, vaccination and licensing. While the woman waited at the hospital for stitches and shots, her friend walked the neighborhood to see if anyone knew the dog in question. A man rushed up eager to report, "No, no, *está bien,* I know the man who owns that dog," and they found the owner and the animal's health certificate. Another story did not end so well. A young woman, a college student who had come for a month of intensive language study and who had such a timid bearing that I wondered how she had ever had the nerve to travel so far alone, told of visiting the U.S. embassy to attend to the matter of having lost her tourist card. While she had sat in the consul's office waiting for advice, she listened to the official talking on the phone. A woman from New York had called, the daughter of a man who had died of a heart attack while traveling in the area. She wanted to bring her father's remains and possessions home. The consul apologized, trying to explain why it had taken a week from the time of his death for her to be notified. Her father had died in a remote area, and before anyone had identified the body, robbers had taken his wallet, watch, clothes and shoes. "Yes," the official tried to explain, "this kind of thing is common . . . you must understand . . . we have done what we could . . ." Then, laying the phone down on his shoulder a moment to address the horrified young woman who sat across from his desk, "Don't worry, you're not going to go to jail."

Among the travelers there was much talk about the water, the rituals of protection to which each adhered: no ice, drink from the bottle not the glass, eat nothing with a skin that has not been cooked, no salad, no leafy garnish, brush teeth with bottled water, be careful about small wounds that open the body to invasion, never eat food from street vendors. Some thought that eating from vendors was safer—no contaminated kitchen counter or utensils. I had called the Centers for Disease Control hotline prior to leaving and listened to the warnings about cholera, malaria, hepatitis A, dengue fever, tuberculosis and polio in Mexico. And there was Montezuma's Revenge, the violent intestinal response to foreign colonization that was the least of the microbial threats, but one that could profoundly disrupt one's faith in the primal sacrament of eating, as I would come to attest. My education in understanding the fundamental terms of privilege continued on the streets. Sidewalks were marked with splatter prints of vomit, urine and loose feces, and sewers vented up a sweet, sickening reek. I began to wonder about taking showers, the offending water rivering over my lips and rinsing my cuticles, nervously chewed raw. I am not a hypochondriac, but I understand the vulnerabilities of the body, how welcoming its warmth is to microorganisms in need of a home.

At the Saturday market a temporary city stakes ground on the southern edge of Oaxaca, block after block, aisle after aisle, of hawkers, buyers and gawkers. Plenty of people just come for the anonymous company of one another, and I became one of them. An old peasant woman tended a clutch of weanling pigs, each tied to the next with a loop of baling twine wrapped around a hind leg. Young goats bleated and stirred restlessly in the crowd. Macaws and parakeets squawked and gurgled. An ancient, shawled brown woman carried two fluffy young turkeys, one tucked under each of her arms. Women rolled string cheese into balls, rolled cloth into head rings to carry wide baskets of bread, chiles, gardenias and roses. Ribbons of intestine, tripe, pigs' feet, dead chickens hung like awnings around meat stands, a severed pig's head displayed prominently like a neon sign. Children milled in the crowd hawking chapulines from a bowl—crispy grasshoppers fried with chile and lime. People bought a few hunks of meat and vegetables, had them grilled on the spot by a woman tending a wood fire, then sat at communal tables to eat amid the market's hubbub.

The avenue of plastic tumblers and household gadgets led to the avenue of leather and cheap clothes. The alley of banana leaves, calla lilies and squash flowers turned into the alley of splayed, salted fish and dried shrimp. An aisle of dazzling Zapotec rugs stood back to back with one of knives and machetes etched with Mayan glyphs or sayings: "Love is like coffee; it must be imbibed while steaming." Mountains of dried chiles stood under slapdash canopies; heaps of zucchinis, oranges and papayas so abundant they did not look like food, but like sculpture, ecstatic geometries of color. Breads and cakes took up a city block. Inflated metallic balloons—lavender bunny, Mickey Mouse, green Ninja turtle, silver unicorn—floated on leashes or rested in hedgerows along the street. A man squatting on a low stool cut hunks of a huge phallic root, explaining the curative properties to a dozen men gathered in a clearing around him. Pyramids of tomatoes, chrysanthemums and papered tomatillos dwarfed the women sitting beside them on the sidewalk, their feet bared and blackened with dirt that seemed to have seeped for a lifetime into their leathery skin.

In the way that a river finds its way through rocks and hills, following a course that has been followed for centuries, people have found their way from the mountains and valleys surrounding Oaxaca to this marketplace. They came first by foot and by donkey, then by pickup truck and bus, everyone there to be part of the milling of people and goods that is among the oldest habits of civilization, though one breaking fast in a world where one can buy anything one wants at any time with no sense that only today are the calabaza blossoms perfect, only today is the vendor of black clay pots or carved wooden jaguars in town, only today is the medicine of the forest available in the city.

I used to feel hassled by the vendors, suckered in by hucksters, unable to ignore the come-on, but too uncomfortable with the language and the teasing rituals of bargaining to enjoy the exchange. I worried that I would be the butt of their jokes, paying dearly for something they had gotten cheap—a stupid American who did not know the value of money, a wealthy American who did not know the price of being poor. I used to think that all I was good for in the teasing transaction of bargaining was my money, and I resented that. But as my Spanish improved, I began to read the market differently, to appreciate how faces brightened with the energy of commerce, how bargaining in this context is a form of friendship, an exchange that prolongs the interaction between strangers, one in which each must ritually express her respect for the value of the other.

There is an air of intimate secrecy with which a woman unfolds for me what she wants me to believe is her finest embroidered tablecloth. *Mucho trabajo,* she says with an earnest and knowing look. Yes, yes, *mucho trabajo. ¿Cuanto cuesta?* And of course the price means nothing to me, but I must act as if it is absurdly high. And she fingers the stitching of the flowered border. *Señora, mire. Mucho trabajo,* begging my womanly sympathy for her days of labor. She may tell me exactly how many days of labor were entailed, and it too will be an absurdly high number. *Sí, sí, es muy bonito. Pero no tengo mucho dinero.* And I make an offer that she must pretend is absurdly low. And then I shake my head sadly to suggest how much I want the lovely tablecloth but cannot afford it, and I begin to walk away. She lets the silence last only a moment, as if it is an elastic holding us together that she does not want to risk stretching too tightly. *Señora, mire. ¿Le gusta esta?* And she holds out a vastly inferior item that does not please me, but allows the elastic to draw us back to one another. And so it goes, each of us prolonging the process, until I leave with the tablecloth and she tucks my money into her pocket. If the transaction is really prolonged, one or other of us might say, *Estás muy duro,* admiring one another's ability to sustain her position while making a compromise.

In the Valley of Oaxaca, "market" has not lost it social meaning as a place and time of gathering. Both the origin of this meaning and the reason it still lives lie in the land. Like much of Mexico, Oaxaca is geographically diverse. The Cocos Plate and North American Plate meet along the west coast of Mexico with sufficient tension to cause ongoing uplifting and earthquakes on the mainland. That activity, over eons, has made the state of Oaxaca environmentally complicated, a buckled and folded density of valleys and mountains. Even though the region is a mere seventeen degrees north of the equator—the same latitude as southern India, Thailand and central Africa—its climate is tropical only in isolated pockets. Along the Pacific coast the weather is hot and desert dry. In the cloud forests facing the Gulf of Mexico it is hot and jungle humid. The highland valleys remain temperate. The central Valley of Oaxaca is a Y-shaped oasis of flatland in the middle of this vast and rugged turmoil of mountains that rise to ten thousand feet and fall into numerous microregions segregated from one another by harsh terrain. Communities that formed in this terrain were isolated from one another, leading to the emergence of the sixteen distinct ethnolinguistic groups that have inhabited the region since before the Conquest.

Not until this century was very much known about pre-Spanish Mexico. The Aztecs told the Spanish conquistadors and missionaries that they had been preceded by people called the Toltecs, and before that gods and other ancestors had inhabited the land. They said that the world had been created and destroyed four times, that they were living in the fifth age, doomed like the others to annihilation. They spoke of the great ruined city of Teotihuacán, where the gods had met to create the present world.

Early in the twentieth century, excavation in the Valley of Mexico confirmed the existence of Teotihuacán and below it the remains of earlier pottery makers. Anthropologist Michael D. Coe writes that by midcentury radiocarbon dating began to fill in the chronology for the fifteen to twenty-four thousand years of Native American history in Mexico. While much detail remains to be learned, the general theory is that early migrants came to the area from Asia, hunted large now-extinct game (mastodon, mammoth, dire wolf), as well as abundant white-tailed deer and collared peccary. Around nine thousand years ago people began to domesticate food plants, probably beginning with the bottle gourd. Recently seeds have been found in a Mexican cave suggesting maize and bean cultivation as early as ten thousand years ago, about the same time that agricultural practices were taking root in the Near East and China. The taming of plants led to a more settled village life, which in turn led to the growth of the first great cities of North America. Twenty-seven centuries before the Spanish arrived, the Olmecs of Veracruz marked their ground with colossal sculpted heads. Roughly a thousand years later, farther north in Mexico, the planned citiesof Teotihuacán and Monte Albán arose with temples, palaces, ball courts and astronomical observatories, and the Zapotecs of the Oaxaca Valley devised the earliest-known writing system in Mesoamerica. Elaborate death customs and artworks evolved; large market centers and trade networks grew;

and hierarchy replaced the egalitarianism of earlier village life.

Seashells from the coast were traded inland, and wooden poles from the mountain forests were traded to the barren flatlands. Because crops growing in widely diverse climatic zones were harvested at different times, no one region could become self-sufficient and cyclical markets developed—a pattern still extant in the valley today. The mineral lore of distinct locales was also exchanged. Oaxacan villagers obtained obsidian from sources hundreds of miles away, trading it from village to village—roughly a day's walk—in a slow relay of local exchanges. Craftsmen in San José Mogote, near Oaxaca, fashioned magnetite into thumbnail-sized mirrors, mounted them in wooden or shell frames to be worn as pendants and traded them with communities as far away as Morelos and the Gulf coast of Veracruz.

Exchanges between villages involved not only goods, but techniques of pottery making and agriculture. A group of symbols— jaguar, caiman, eagle—leaked across cultural boundaries. Sculptural motifs similar to the Olmecs' great basalt heads appeared in stone figurines in the Valley of Oaxaca. These communities, from the most remote antiquity, wove a cultural pattern in which local differences were the warp and weft, and the land was the loom on which it was woven.

A traveler is not an archaeologist or historian, but her piecemeal assembling of an order out of the chaos of experience is not unlike the process employed by those specialists. A traveler sets out uncertain what she will find and enlivened by that uncertainty. She gathers evidence for a theory that adds up to little more than her personal joy. The world is new to her, is true to her senses and imagination, and she lays her mind open to it. She keeps traveling in order to keep discovering the edge of her ignorance, for she loves nothing more than the moment of overcoming her ignorance, no matter how briefly. Travel satisfies because it so closely mirrors the journey of a life: one begins at home and must leave and learn to feel at home in the chaos of the world's foreignness and danger.

On this journey I vowed to myself two things: to learn enough Spanish not to fear traveling alone in Mexico and to broaden my sense of what it means to be an American. I wanted to see my privilege in a broader context and not take my comforts for granted. I wanted to feel my sense of culture deepen. For it seemed that at home my culture, while being responsible for so much of the technological advance that defines civilization, had become trivial and mean, self-interested and self-aggrandizing, and had left me feeling socially maladjusted and spiritually bereft. The privilege of individual freedom, for which people all over the world still hungered and risked their lives, had dissipated in the United States from an idea of social justice to one of personal wealth. Rather than feeling a passion about their citizenship in the world's great democracy, most U.S. citizens distrusted their government, their schools, their religions, their scientists, their artists, and even their families—indeed all the institutions that constitute genuine culture—and had retreated from this newly dangerous chaos into the elaborate distractions of entertainment and wealth. Paz says that the North American is lost in the world of inhuman objects he has made and cannot recognize himself, while the Mexican, being viscerally connected to the Conquest as mestizo, is "torn from the center of creation and suspended between hostile forces" trying "to reestablish the bonds that unite us to the universe."

One evening in Oaxaca I stood on the hotel roof, where sheets and towels billowed on the clothesline. An afternoon rain had made the cobblestones shine and kept the laundry outside. Dogs and goats and fireworks again peppered the quiet. Two huge, sprawling coquito trees—the only ones of such size, I was told, in all the Oaxaca Valley—canopied the church courtyard next door. Families began to arrive for a wedding, all the generations dressed in their best and looking serious. An imperfect, yet dignified, mariachi band played the processional. During the ceremony the sanctuary doors stayed open, even though a stray dog kept running in, only to be escorted out again and again. All the precision and efficiency of the technological North seemed useless here. Music and prayer streamed out of the sanctuary and into the street, eddying together into one current.

Monte Albán no longer exists as a city. Now it is a high and grassy ruin of stone. But for a thousand years or so it was the center of the world for the residents of the Oaxaca Valley. On a hot January day I joined a VW bus tour and rode out of Oaxaca's bustle, past shantytowns of sheet-metal cubicles into the parched and open countryside. Our group included two Colombians, two Costa Ricans, two Italians, Eduardo, our Mexican guide who spoke a little Italian and less English, and me. This turned out to be to my advantage, because Eduardo took pity on me as the linguistic outsider and promised to speak slowly for me. When we stopped in Tule to see the widest tree in the world, a cypress two thousand years old, he sat beside me in the shade while the others bustled for photos, and he helped me spell out in my notebook *ahuehuetl,* the Nahuatl word for cypress, then *árbol de agua.* The exchange was not entirely linguistic. I was the only single woman in the group, and since Eduardo's two teenage sons had come along, his attentions began to feel like a display of polite and harmless courtship behavior for their benefit.

We drove on to the ruins, the Colombians and Costa Ricans comparing the cost of living, food, bargaining conventions in various Latin American countries they had visited—I understood the form of their exchange, if not the content. As we spiraled up the mountainside, the sea of arid pastures with habitations clustered on islands of green fell below us. We were heading for the uninhabited heights. The sun was rarefied at this altitude, the light dramatic, as if every detail had been staged in order to impress an audience: the single white blossom of the morning glory shrub, the thorned blade of agave, the blue haze of distant mountains, the broad bare sky that offered no comfort, only a clarity of scale that made us shrink beneath it. When I stepped out into the parking lot, I felt transparent and glad for the gauntlet of vendors selling cold bottled water and straw hats that smelled of fresh-cut grass.

Our group split in two for Spanish or English language tours. I was exhausted from the effort at understanding and made the easy choice, heading off with a new group in the company of an archaeology student from Mexico City. He led us to an area of underground tombs, each locked with a steel hatch. Graffiti and pissing, he explained. There were 280 tombs, he said, a hundred of them found in excavations during the past few years. We were in luck, he said, because today one tomb was open. He led us down the steep stairs into the cold, stone dark. Once everyone was crowded inside, a man standing outside tipped a sheet of cardboard covered with aluminum foil to direct sunlight into the tomb. Behind a wrought-iron grate stood a few red pottery figurines and in a niche above our heads hung a stone mask of the rain god wearing a quetzal headdress. A turquoise, pearl and gold pectoral had been found in this tomb, the guide explained, but it was now in a museum for safekeeping, along with most of the city's artifacts. He said that sometimes the dead had been buried with a living dog or human companions to help on the difficult journey to the land of the dead. In some tombs one skeleton had been found; in others, seven or nine. Sometimes, he said, there had been scratch marks on the walls where a companion had tried to get out.

By the time we emerged back into the light a few campesinos had gathered outside. One took me aside, whispering a confidence as he unwrapped the rags protecting a walnut-sized carving he had pulled from his pocket. It was a stone head wearing an intricate glyphlike serpent mask. He rewrapped it and pulled out another—an effigy of the rain god. He was one of three men who dogged our party, sidling up, speaking softly and urgently to one of us—this is a bargain, a treasure, available only to you. The guide said they were farmers who worked the surrounding fields and had permission to sell artifacts they found there, though they also sold newly made replicas, without telling the buyer the difference. The valley is dotted with archaeological sites, hundreds of them as yet unexplored, such as the adjacent hilltop, Monte Albán Chico, where, our guide reported, one could often find the fresh feathers and blood of Indian ritual.

The campesino unwrapped a black stone jaguar head, nudged my arm and urged me, *"Mire."* "Is this Zapotec?" I asked the man, who handed me the rough two-inch-tall figure. *"Sí, sí, Zapoteca."* Zapotecs had built Monte Albán, though my question told me nothing about whether the piece was artifact or replica. Zapotecs continue to inhabit the valley and are among its most successful entrepreneurs, having developed an international market with Pier One and Bloomingdale's for their weavings. "Is it very old?" I asked. *"Sí, muy antigua."* I wanted the creature to have slept deep in fertile soil for a thousand years, wanted my touch to awaken its potency.

"Women use the jaguar in their medicine," he said. "It has powers."

I later read that the ancient Zapotecs believed their fate was linked to an animal with whom they shared a personal fate. If their animal was wounded or died in a particular manner, so too would the person. And if a bad fate befell the person, so too would it befall the animal. Zapotecs were brave because they considered themselves the offspring of wild beasts. But at the time, I did not know this. I was interested in the object because of this earnest man who knew nothing about me, but knew how to win my interest.

The jaguar was crudely carved, wore ear spools and a woven headband. Its teeth were bared in a mean grimace, but its eyes remained focused and calm. The carving had been broken unevenly at the neck, yet stood flat enough to rest on my palm. It had none of the cloying perfection of a mass-market souvenir. And I began to feel that it did have power, whether carved in the last year or the last millennium. We settled the bargain as we walked slowly from the tombs to the plaza, lagging behind the group. When I rejoined them, several teased me as if I had been ripped off and deceived, but I was as happy to think about the power of my ten dollars in the farmer's hands as I was to have the jaguar, even if powerless, in mine.

The guide had mounted the steps overlooking the grand plaza where monumental geometric structures of stone—stepped pyramids, foundation grids and cobbled remnant walls—lay before us. We looked closely at the stonework noting where mortared pebbles signaled that reconstruction had been done. The floors and walls once were covered with mica, others plastered then painted with vegetable and mineral dyes. One building had a chamber admitting sunlight only at one time in the year—the official calendar indicating when to plant crops. Water was carried up the mountain or captured as sparse rain and dispersed in an elaborate cistern-and-duct system. Another building was lined with stone tablets, each depicting an enemy turned upside down on his head. These "conquest tablets" served as another type of calendar, measuring the city's history by the increments of its political victories.

Monte Albán was the capital of a valley-wide Zapotec state. Its population totaled thirty to sixty thousand in the year 600, its heyday roughly contemporaneous with that of the great city of Teotihuacán in the Valley of Mexico. The ancient Zapotecs had two names for their city, one meaning "fortress" and the other "sacred mountain." "Zapotec," meaning "the people of the zapote," a black fruit, is the name the Aztecs gave these people. By 700 or so Monte Albán was abandoned; it was later occupied by the Mixtecs, "people of the clouds." All of this took place hundreds of years before the Aztecs, the fiercest people ever to live in Mexico, arrived from the north to expand their empire. No one knows why the Zapotecs left their sacred city. Probably a prolonged drought, combined with earthquakes, disease, food and water shortages, ruined their urban way of life.

Whatever their reasons for walking away from Monte Albán, the Zapotecs were among the first people on earth to know that, as Edward Sapir wrote, civilization may move ever on, but cultures rise and fall. "The genuine culture," he writes,

> *is not of necessity either high or low; it is merely inherently harmonious, balanced, self-satisfactory. It is the expression of a richly varied and yet somehow unified and consistent attitude toward life, an attitude which sees the significance of any one element of civilization in its relation to all others. It is, ideally speaking, a culture in which nothing is spiritually meaningless.*

We walked to the ballcourt, a grassy I-shaped clearing lined with stone bleachers. The ancient ball games were religious contests, a battle between the forces of good and evil, light and dark. In some parts of ancient Mexico the game was played to the death. Stelae from Yucatán depict the winner holding up the severed head of the loser like a flag. Our guide thought that human sacrifice was not a part of Zapotec culture, that here the loser might have had to give up jewelry or clothing. Some researchers believe that animal sacrifice played a part in the culture's rituals.

There is no reason to level off a mountain top and build a city, without aid of draft animals, wheel, metal tools or easy water, except power: to exploit your power over those beneath you and to court the powers that lie above. Maintaining power requires vision: the physical ability to see the enemy coming and the metaphysical ability to see the forces beyond your control that may swing your fate. The systems of politics and faith that guided the flourishing of Monte Albán remain encoded in written language that has not yet been decoded. Though Zapotec is still widely spoken in the Valley of Oaxaca, its early written version, part glyph and part image, remains one of the world's last undeciphered languages. The fruits of political conquest must have helped to foster the higher aspects of Zapotec culture. It is likely that slaves, perhaps Mixtec war prisoners, built the palaces, temples, tombs and water ducts, freeing up time for the elite to pursue art, religion and science. But as those higher pursuits evolved, it seems likely that some reflection about the injustice of this method of cultural advance must have emerged, some crack in the sense of order, that allowed chaos to enter in.

There are no adequate words for the mystery of lost cultures. One is attracted and repulsed by them, visits museums to stare at the artifacts in disbelief of their beauty or horror: the trophy skull with two small holes drilled in the top to hang it as an ornament; another skull encrusted with turquoise chips, carved white seashell doughnuts for the eyeholes; the human mandible etched with glyphs, a serpent's head where the mouth should be, human teeth still in their sockets. The guide said priests wore the mandibles as masks to scare people. I remembered a day or two earlier having stood before one in the Rufino Tamayo Museum, thinking of the hours the mandible had turned in the hands of the craftsman, the likelihood that he had known the warrior or priest or enemy from whose head the bone had been cut. "Wonderful, no?" said the elegant Mexican woman who had stood long beside me, both of us stuck on the thing. "Yes," I said, shaken to find myself admiring the spiritual power of something so gruesome. "Yes," I agreed, "wonderful."

The Aztecs are the pre-Columbian culture about which we know the most, because the sixteenth-century conquistadors and missionaries documented, while destroying and converting, the culture they found in Mexico. The portrait they drew emphasizes the bloodlust and savagery of the Aztecs: mass rituals of human sacrifice, the flaying and donning of human skins, the ripping of beating hearts from human chests, and the ritual eating of human flesh. As brutal as the Aztecs may have been, many historians now believe that the Spanish accounts were exaggerated, because for the colonizers to see the indigenous people as monstrously savage helped to justify their own brutality. Tzvetan Todorov paints the broad strokes:

> *Without going into detail, and merely to give a general idea (even if we do not feel entirely justified in rounding off figures when it is a question of human lives), it will be*

recalled that in 1500 the world population is approxi-
mately 400 million, of whom 80 million inhabit the Amer-
icas. By the middle of the sixteenth century, out of these 80
million, there remain 10. Or limiting ourselves to Mexico:
on the eve of the conquest, its population is about 25 mil-
lion; in 1600, it is one million.

Nevertheless, Michael Coe writes, "the main goal of the Aztec state was war." Their war songs convey the sense of purpose and duty that battle inspired: "The battlefield is the place: / where one toasts the divine liquor of war."

We may see the Aztecs as less civilized than ourselves, but they were arguably more cultured, for their brutality had spiritual meaning. They saw their relationship with death as active and participatory. To earn life they believed they must feed life to their gods. "That is why we see sacrificial victims," writes Todorov, "accepting their lot, if not with joy, in any case without despair; and the same is true of soldiers on the battlefield: their blood will help keep the society alive." Often the victims were given drugs on the eve of their sacrifice to help them uphold this ideal, for despair would be a bad omen at the time of sacrifice. The souls of warriors who died by the priest's blade or on the battlefield went not the Land of the Dead, but to the Paradise of the Sun God.

The Aztecs developed a complex mythology and religion. Their calendar meshed an almanac year of 260 days, a solar year of 365 days, and the 584-day synodic period of Venus. Their religious devotion was expressed not only in battle and human sacrifice, but also in ritual speeches and poems, called "flower songs." Consider these words, ritually spoken by the midwife after cutting the newborn's umbilical cord:

Oh my dear child, oh my jewel, oh my quetzal feather,
you have come to life, you have been born, you have come
out of the earth. Our lord created you, fashioned you,
caused you to be born upon the earth, he by whom all live,
God. We have awaited you, we who are your mothers,
your fathers; and your aunts, your uncles, your relatives
have awaited you; they wept, they were sad before you
when you came to life, when you were born upon the
earth.

In 1519, Coe reports, the Aztecs may have been the only people in the world with universal schooling for both sexes. Their leaders served as the warriors, as engineers overseeing great urban construction projects, and as philosopher/poets. This flower song was composed by the fifteenth-century king of Texcoco:

I, Nezahualcoyotl, ask this:
Is it true one really lives on the earth?
Not forever on earth,
only a little while here.
Though it be jade it falls apart,
though it be gold it wears away.
Not forever on earth,
only a little while here.

The oldest tablets at Monte Albán are called the Dancers. Some stand propped against stone footings of long-gone buildings. Others form a wall with figures cut in low relief. A row of swimmers drift musically across a horizontal plane between rows of dancers—larger tablets depicting upright figures—standing, squatting, kneeling, fetally curved, with an arm bent behind the head or with wildly twisted legs. Some figures appear more than once. Some wear ear spools and elaborate necklaces. Some appear to be deformed, or to have suffered genital mutilation (a circle cut, for example, in place of a penis). There are a hunchback, a breech birth, and a woman who appears to have died in childbirth. Some images bear inscriptions in unreadable word glyphs; others bear time glyphs. Numbers appear as bars and dots.

The figures were once thought to be ceremonial dancers, but too many of them look contorted and deformed to satisfy that theory. Other interpreters have suggested that the alternating small horizontal and large vertical figures represent subjugation and domination, that the tablets record the Zapotec history of political conflicts. But that theory too seems inadequate, because the "subjugated" figures swim blissfully, while the "dominators" look physically deformed. A more recent theory proposes that the tablets served as a medical encyclopedia, that the building where they were found was a medical school. This theory suits our current bent for reading archaic cultures in a more dignified light than did previous generations, for science today carries a higher cultural valence than does dancing. For now, in deference to tradition or poetry or the longing for a more lyrical world, the figures continue to be called the Dancers.

There are words for lost cultures, but they speak mostly about ourselves. Surely they were more savage than we are, we think, proud of how civilized we have become. Surely we have lost their visceral closeness to nature, we think, sorry at how civilized we have become. We forgive ourselves a little on both counts, wishing we knew a little less history and a little more meaning. We wonder how we will be remembered if anyone is around a thousand years from now to do the job. We are not sure that we believe in the human future, though we live in the most advanced civilization the Earth has known. The deeper in history we live, the more we live in a basic condition of self-doubt. Sapir writes, "It would be idle to praise or blame any fundamental condition of our civilization, to praise or blame any strand in the warp and woof of its genius. These conditions and these strands must be accepted as basic."

chapter 7

Wattle and Daub

Eduardo enjoyed the afternoon of touring the ruins, I think, more than any of the tourists. It gave his flamboyance a playing field. He would give us the facts, then announce, "The widest tree in the world!" like a circus barker who knows he sounds like a parody of a circus barker. He wanted to complete our cultural education by taking us to a mescal distillery. And so we drove into the Tlacolula Valley through which the Pan American Highway wobbles on its way east out of Oaxaca heading toward Santiago, Chile. The Sierra Madres, fractured into two chains, rose to the south and north of us, grand distant presences that made what lay between them feel cozy—an alluvial plain, a few rough clumps of cultivated castor bean trees with wine red stalks, scattered wild mesquite and agave, a sandy white arroyo cut with the curves of water's earlier passage, rolling blanched grass hills that had never had the chance to drink their fill. A handful of children tended a small herd of goats and cows in a fenceless cornfield. The animals were gleaning the sparse remains of desiccated stalks, and their bony haunches did not look much more promising than the bare-dirt field.

Everyone in the VW bus was game for the distillery. Mescal is the national drink of Mexico, touted as the preventive for *la turista* (the intestinal terror we in our north-of-the-border humor call Montezuma's Revenge) and an aphrodisiac. Women prefer it,

Eduardo coaxed, *suave con frutas.* Never having been shy to acknowledge my preferences, I said I liked mine straight up. We
toured the plant, which was much too clean for any real work.
The agave was crushed under a huge medieval millstone, then
cooked outdoors with hot stones in a pit, then fermented in a
wooden vat the size of a hot tub, and finally distilled in a gleaming industrial-scale copper still. Samples were lined up for us at
the bar. We all tried a brand called Machos.

"An aphrodisiac!" promised Eduardo. "Drink this and you
will have five children, six children, *ten children!*" He was ebul-
lient, though that wasn't *my* idea of an aphrodisiac. He told me
the Nahuatl word for children, a funny word, we agreed. And
then the men started popping down gusanos, the agave worms
bottled with mescal. These were laid out in a straw basket, dozens
of them, which the men dipped in salt and swallowed whole.
None of the women partook.

"They're very clean," bartender encouraged me, but I was not
convinced. Then all the men started teasing all the women to try
them.

After three shots, one of Eduardo's teenage sons asked me if I
was "seasick." I had been delighted to learn *modismos* from my
Spanish teacher in Oaxaca. What would be the equivalent of our
"Cool!" I had asked. "*¡Que padre!*" he answered. Or if something
was *totally* cool, "*¡Padrísimo!*" He told us words used as expressions of surprise in different Mexican regions. "*¡Caracoles!*" (literally, "Snails!") was in some locales the equivalent of the more
familiar "*¡Ay caramba!*" The utter rightness of these words and
the impossibility of translating them literally was fascinating to
me. The etymological journey that had brought such expressions into current usage would be intriguing to revisit. I realized,
shaking my head in confusion at Eduardo's son, that we had
stumbled off the trail of such a journey.

"Are you *drunk?*" Eduardo clarified, one of the few good English words he had. His son then gestured for me to join him near the millstone, where a pitchfork leaned against a vat of pulverized fermenting agave. He asked me, through gesture and facial expression, for the English word for the implement, and when I gave it to him he forced his mouth to shape the alien consonants, then wrote the word in his notebook, adding it to a long, carefully inscribed list. He asked me for a word for "drunk" that he could use with the tourists. I hesitated, considering the range of possibilities. The most commonly used choices—"shit-faced" and "fucked up"—weren't appropriate, when I considered him asking a sedate group of retirees. "Tipsy," I finally suggested. "Are you tipsy?" And I imitated someone who has lost her equilibrium from drinking. They were very happy to have this word, a funny word, and kept repeating it to one another and laughing on the ride back to the city, rehearsing their next tour on which they would delight the sedate group of retirees from the North by asking, "Are you tipsy?"

Eduardo dropped us off in the zócalo, and we exchanged phone numbers, promising to get together to teach one another more *modismos.* The zócalo is the heart of the city, and I never tired of being there. I ate at its sidewalk cafés whenever I could and lingered to watch the sun freckling through the grand copal trees and people circulating in Oaxaca's bloodstream—beggars, German and Japanese tourists, shoeshine men and flower women, the pizza delivery boy on his scooter, the blind singer with his battered two-string guitar, children selling Chiclets and worthless Taiwanese toys, the zócalo boys on the hustle for money or sex, whichever came first, and local families out for a walk. Always the sunlight was electric with intensity.

On this afternoon an oompah version of "On the Street Where You Live" spilled from the white wrought-iron bandstand. Protesters chanted and waved banners outside the governor's palace, demanding recourse for their village, where an election had been held that "was no election." The palace remained silent, stone-faced soldiers standing guard. The square and side streets were lined with vendors' stalls for Christmas week, a string of kiddie rides set up beside the cathedral. There were stalls where you could buy traditional clothing—embroidered *huipils* and *trajes* that stylistically identified their makers as Trique, Quiche or Mayan. There were stalls where you could buy a ceramic plate and throw it backward over your shoulder against the cathedral wall for good luck in the New Year.

I found a quiet corner café and ordered black beans and a quesadilla. The beans tasted of anise, and I learned from the waiter that they had been cooked with avocado leaves, an Oaxacan specialty. Beggars and vendors dogged my table—scruffy children and ancient women leaning close with practiced expressions of need. An old man who seemed to lack a keel stumbled among the tables, carrying a coffee tin and sticking a fake gun in people's ribs. The gun was made of white one-inch plumber's pipe, masking tape, and a dirty chunk of two-by-four. He staged a mock holdup at each table, then smiled and laughed and raised up his beggar's can. At the table next to me a group of young men who looked like U.S. college students were tossing down beers and comparing guidebooks. The gunman went for one guy's back, and the guy twitched him off like a fly. The beggar made a second approach, this time placing his gun against the young man's neck. This time the young man bristled and threatened. The joke had gone on too long. I'll never forget that old man's face, submissive and coy, toying with male aggression to get what he needed. An entrepreneur among beggars, part thief and part entertainer, he had carved for himself a market niche in a very competitive field.

The institute where I was studying Spanish had arranged for me to move out of my hotel and live with a local family for a few weeks. I knew it would be a humbling and educational experience. The basic daily requirement for communication in a home would force me beyond the pallid Spanish I had so far mustered. Nevertheless, I stalled as the hour for my move approached, knowing that I would surely make a fool of myself numerous times and hoping that my hosts would be gracious and forgiving enough not to take lasting offense at my verbal blunders. No matter how welcoming my hosts might be, I knew I would remain an outsider, unable to perceive the place from inside its culture. That would take a few generations. I had two weeks. Ironically, while tradition at home may feel oppressive—a sea chest loaded with the worn-out assumptions of the past—tradition in someone else's culture is the difference we hunger for.

I rang the bell at the gate of the walled house on a quiet side street south of the zócalo. A teenage girl ran up the cement walk to let me in. She was at the stage of development I remembered well from my daughter's adolescence, her body just beginning to define itself as womanly. She ran with the awkwardness of one who still knows herself to be a little girl, but whose body has begun to disagree. This stage reminded me of the time my daughter was first noticed in an overtly sexual way by a man. A stranger had whistled at her on the street, and she came home flummoxed, unable to comprehend what had invited that attention. The barred gate swung open, the girl reached for my bags, and la señora of the house, an elderly and sensible-looking woman, followed smiling up the walk.

"We've been expecting you!" she enthused, embracing me and kissing both cheeks. Our first confused conversation ensued about my arrival time, how they had not been sure what day I was coming, since I had started out in a hotel. Neither of them spoke English, but Rosa Elena Limón routinely hosted students and emitted an eager confidence that we would understand each other. I was immediately grateful for her common sense in this regard, making me all the more committed not to violate her hospitality.

The house was modest, a few steps rising to a cement veranda graced with a narrow settee, pastoral paintings by Rosa Elena's daughter, and three bird cages housing burbling blue-and-yellow parakeets. The exterior wall had been painted with streaks of deep turquoise smeared against a white background. The effect suggested water or sky, or some reflecting combination of the two. Inside there was not much of a living room—a small dark corner with a few formal-looking upholstered chairs. The center of the house was a big wooden table covered with a plastic-lace tablecloth that filled the dining room. It looked out into a small drab courtyard with a birdbath. The large sideboard was crowded with family photos, Christmas cards and an elaborate nativity scene with dozens of figurines and winking white lights. My room was in the basement, as comfortable as I required but no more so. It had a double bed, an armoire for my clothes, a little table for books. It was damp and cool, with a narrow window near the ceiling that looked out on some leggy geraniums in the front courtyard. I nodded my approval, and Rosa Elena invited me back upstairs for something to eat. Though it was late in the afternoon, and I was stuffed from lunch, I did not refuse.

A place was set for me at the table. I had not expected this, having signed on to eat only breakfasts at their home. What with the confusion about my arrival, it seemed the place must have been set for days. Rosa Elena sat across from me, arms crossed comfortably around her ample chest, smiling and nodding and perking up her eyebrows for my approval as Elvira, her god-daughter, delivered course after course. First, a bowl of clear chicken broth with morsels of carrot, green bean and rice. Did I like chile? she asked. Yes, yes, I replied. Our cooking is very Mexican at home in Arizona. Her face warmed. Elvira brought me a small bowl of green but fiery tomatillo sauce that I spooned into my soup. Next came a single, slender crepa rolled with bits of chicken and ham. It was crispy and delicate, no bigger than a stout peapod. Then came a chunk of roasted beef with thin tomato sauce and two round potatoes the size of Ping-Pong balls, with side dishes of black beans and fresh corn tortillas wrapped in a paper napkin to keep them warm. The beans, once again, had a flavor of anise that made me linger with every bite. By the time the flan arrived with its rusty drizzle of burnt sugar, I was as stuffed as a sausage.

"What do you like to eat for breakfast?" she asked.

"Usually cereal and coffee," I answered, beginning to fear her generosity, and feeling stupid for being able to speak only in utilitarian phrases. The conversation was for me like trying to see through fog, occasional gusts of wind blowing clear a line of sight.

"Would cornflakes with milk be okay?"

"Yes, that would be fine."

"We'll buy some, but tomorrow would you like queso con chile?"

"Oh, I'd love that," I replied, suddenly realizing that asking for cornflakes for breakfast in Oaxaca was like asking for a Navajo taco in New York City. "Yes, I'd like to try the foods Oaxacans eat."

Rosa Elena encouraged me to rest for a while, and then, she promised, we would go for a walk. I sank gratefully into the cool silence of my room.

· · ·

"Architecture is a society's unbribable witness," writes Paz. And it is true that the remains of the sky city of Monte Albán bear testimony to its founding culture. But food too is a conduit of culture. Two thousand years ago the Zapotecs ate corn tortillas. We know this because the clay griddles, or *comales,* on which tortillas continue to be cooked on the streets of Oaxaca were found in all households of the valley dating from the village stage that preceded Monte Albán. "Maize was and is the very basis of settled life in Mexico," writes Michael Coe, "and, in fact, throughout the regions of the New World civilized in pre-Columbian times." Pollen grains taken from fossil cores dug in the Valley of Oaxaca suggest that wild maize was in Mexico at least eighty thousand years ago, predating any human presence there. How the small wild progenitor became the New World's most important plant remains unknown. There are many theories about where in North or South America the slow process of domestication took place, about what plant or plants actually were the wild progenitors, and about just how the process of capturing the mutations that led to larger cobs and kernels developed. When first cultivated, Coe writes, the maize cobs "were no larger than a strawberry."

To make tortillas, corn is soaked overnight in water with lime, making the kernels swell and soften so they are easier to grind, hull and all, on the metate. The dough is patted into thin disks, then baked on the *comal.* Tortillas are made daily. When moist, they get moldy, but when crisped they last for days or weeks and can be carried by a farmer or traveler.

Early every morning at Rosa Elena's house, while I lay in the last filmy stages of sleep, the bell at her gate would ring. It seemed odd to me that a guest would call so early. Some days her adult daughter, Rosie, would join us for breakfast before going on to her office job. But the bell would have rung whether or not Rosie was with us. Finally one morning I got up early enough to see Elvira run out to the gate to answer the bell and trade some coins for a package of warm, freshly made tortillas. I never did eat cornflakes for breakfast at their home. Every morning I had a plate of sliced papaya, a bowl of thin green chile in which two small slabs of delectable Oaxacan cheese lay submerged, a side dish of black beans flavored with avocado leaf, and a fresh tortilla, while my host sat opposite me nodding with pleasure. I asked her how to make the salsa. It's easy, she said, and she led me into the kitchen, showing me what she called chilitos verdes and the small saucepan in which she boiled them with tomatillos. It sounded simple. But while asking for "little green chiles" at the neighborhood market might produce just what I needed, elsewhere even in Mexico it would be like asking for "little green leaves."

Chiles are indigenous to the region. They are air pollinators and crossbreed so easily that there are over a hundred different types found in Mexico, each with a distinct flavor. All are varieties of *Capsicum annuum*, with the exception of the habañero from Yucatán, which is a different species and the hottest of them all. Local names for chiles change from place to place, and they are often mislabeled, if labeled at all, in the market. Within remote mountainous areas growing conditions can vary dramatically within a few miles. There are chiles grown in Oaxaca found nowhere else in Mexico, such as chilhuacles negros that give the local moles their intensity of flavor and color. The desired culinary properties come not only from the place where the chiles are grown, but also the time of harvest and method of preparation. The justly revered chipotle is an undistinguished-looking shriveled brown thing, produced from a ripened jalapeño that has been dried and then smoked under banana leaves. Its name comes from the Nahuatl: *chil* (chile) plus *potli* (smoke). Indeed, chile peppers are the major ingredient of hot foods in all the world's cuisines, a gift of Mexican and Peruvian origin. Another major American contribution to the world's culinary palette, the tomato, came originally from Peru to Mexico in pre-Columbian times and probably first made its way to Europe on Spanish ships in the fifteenth century. Its name too comes from the Nahuatl: *xicotomatl.*

On one of our walks, Rosa Elena took me to the Benito Juárez Market—the best one in the city for textiles, I thought—and we wandered the dense maze admiring embroidered dresses and tablecloths. Elvira preferred the fantastically painted wooden figurines, especially the snakes. The smells of wood fires in cooking grills, roasting corn, sour meat, putrid dried fish, oregano and thyme and marjoram bundled together (for mole, she explained), sweet squash flowers and gardenias all blended into a rich olfactory stew. Women sold bowls of fresh atole, the ancient Aztec drink made from dried corn, scooped into coconut shells from an open vat that looked gray, murky and undrinkable. I did not dare eat anything in the market—it seemed such a melee of bacterial exchange.

And then there were the chiles. Mounds of them heaped on table after table, fresh and dry, red and green and black, some the size of my pinkie, others the size of my hand, some wrinkled and shrunken, others pristinely smooth. Women breezed among them calling them by name: guajillos, mulatos, poblanos, and the delicate smoky moritas, each with its special use. This one makes salsa for memolitos, this for mole—you *must* have this one for mole; from this one you must remove the seeds, but this one leave the seeds in. They tried out the feel of them in their hands and bought them by the sackful.

.   .   .

On the night I got sick, during one brief interval of sleep, I dreamed I was living in a rustic cabin on the Oregon coast. A man came to visit me, someone who had sparked a romantic flame in me, not a likeness of an actual person, but a dream lover, in this case a field biologist, sturdily built with a trim gray beard. I welcomed him into the wonderful open space in which I lived, one big room with exposed rafters and beams. And then creatures began to climb out of the wooden crossbeams over-head—black-and-yellow organisms that looked like planaria, a shape I remembered from high school biology. More and more of them came out of the walls, and their bodies began to swell. So beautiful were their shapes, so vivid and intense their colors, that we watched them as if they were kites or hot-air balloons. But they kept growing and swelling and filling the air, more and more of them getting born, until we became afraid and were forced to leave the house.

I suppose the biologist in that dream was an aspect of myself that did not suffer the pain and physical revolution of my gas-trointestinal woes. He was interested, sober, attentive, a student of life in all its manifestations. And I loved him for it. There was, however, the everyday aspect of myself that did indeed suffer the pain of that ordeal, which erupted violently in the night, then calmed, or nearly so, and returned in waves of varying in-tensity over the next several months. Whatever organism had launched a population explosion in my gut, it managed to so dis-rupt my capacity to digest that I spent many weeks pleased if I could manage some saltines, chamomile tea or plain rice with-out internal violence.

One tends to take the ability to eat for granted. I was left with the memory of food as consolation, mentally replaying the meals of the past few days, reminding myself that I had no regrets about eating them, and trying to pinpoint the source of my illness. There had been the big meal of pollo con mole negro at Maria Bonito's, one of the city's best restaurants. I had eaten there with a group of friends. We had gorged on a salsa—more like a soupy guacamole with lots of fresh cilantro and lime—that could have violated the "no uncooked vegetables" protocol. But no one else had suffered for it. I could not believe it had been the chiles rellenos I ate the day before at La Casa de Mi Abuela. These were not the fried lumps of batter and cheese one gets in the North, but two rudy pasilla chiles stuffed with minced pork, fruit and nuts, then roasted to a smoky, delicate complexity that made me reach with every mouthful to try to understand the flavor. Finally, I decided the culprit must have been the quesadilla I ate for lunch at a no-name café near the institute. I had so far avoided a local delicacy, flor de calabaza—fresh squash blossoms—cooked into tlayudas or quesadillas on street-corner *comales*. When I saw them on the café's menu and pictured the fragrant baskets of yellow-veined trumpet blossoms I had seen in the market, I could resist no longer. By the time the quesadilla arrived at my table, I wondered if I had made a mistake. Lovely huge sprigs of fresh cilantro poked out of the folded tortilla. The leaves had not even been wilted from the heat that melted the cheese. And inside the fold lay a row of brilliant yellow flowers, softened slightly by the heat, but retaining the shapeliness that promised their fragrance would be palpable. And so it was—an exquisite fecundity on the tongue.

Luckily the trip I had planned with friends from the institute fell on a day when I felt almost healthy. John and Jennie were graduate students, he studying literature at Harvard, she anthropology at Columbia. They were lively and witty and shared my unreasonable love of books, so we had plenty of goods to

exchange. I liked their style of traveling. They would check out
a few facts in the guidebooks, then experiment out into the
world, armed with partial knowledge and eager eyes. I felt more
kinship with these young people than I did with colleagues my
own age who approached traveling with a competence and pro-
fessionalism that left me cold, too much decided ahead of time
about what one's experience would be, too much energy ex-
pended on superlatives—the finest, the oldest, the highest, the
newest—and not enough on absorbing the ordinary in an ex-
traordinary place. I preferred to savor the pleasure of being an
outsider, customs not my own playing out before me so that the
dull business of the day, those things that become tarnished with
use, began to shine.

Two other students from the institute joined us, Josh and Jeff,
scruffy guys in their twenties whom we had jokingly called "the
slackers," but who actually turned out to be adventurers of a sort
and eager to practice their new language skills. Jeff had traveled
to Chile and beyond with no money and no Spanish in order to
climb mountains, and Josh had worked for a hoods-in-the-
woods project in the Pacific Northwest, bringing drug-troubled
teenagers back to their senses through rugged wilderness experiences. All seemed eager to enter into friendship without the hierarchies of generational difference, and so we set out from the
seedy and rank second-class bus station on a battered old Blue
Bird bus. The vehicle was a sorry, groaning mess and bore evidence of its former employment for a U.S. school district in the
form of a Wisconsin bumper sticker and windshield decals that
read, "Let's Party," "McDonald's," and "Don't Worry Be Happy."
A pig and two goats rode on the roof rack. The seats were filled
with locals heading to one village or another. Zapotec women,
their heads wrapped in rebozos, carried bundles of asters and
gladiolas loosely wrapped in newspaper. A woman boarded the

bus with a sackful of cheeping baby chicks. At each village where we stopped a vendor came to the open dusty windows selling Cokes and snacks. At one stop a woman boarded with a grain sack slit in three places through which the heads of gawking turkeys poked. I heard sounds I had never heard before in the greeting that Zapotec women gave to one another, a gravelly-sounding word, as one would lightly touch another's palm with her fingertips, not a handshake, a different custom of greeting, a gentle grazing touch, fingertips along the tenderest part of the palm.

We got off at an intersection in the sere middle of nowhere halfway between Tlacolula and Teotitlán, rolling hills of desiccated mesquite grasslands rising toward the Sierra Madres on both sides of the road. It was a hot, windy morning. We walked a kilometer up the road past children tending a herd of goats and mangy dogs in a stubbled cornfield. The ruins rested on a high island of volcanic tuff above the nearly dry Río Salado and its alluvial plain. The site was quiet. No tour guides, no gauntlet of vendors, no snack bars, no slick brochures. A little birdsong, a little wind were the only disturbances. We were free to roam among the stone walls and mazelike corridors, to sit on stone bleachers lining the barren ballcourt (the largest in the Oaxaca Valley) and photograph the elegant geometric fretwork of stone mosaics. These friezes so finely worked had led archaeologists to believe that the site had been the home for priests and aristocrats. The style, similar to mosaics found at nearby Mitla, was more intricate and ornate than anything at the Zapotec ruins. There was little sense of enormous public architecture, as I had seen at Monte Albán. This was an enclave, a refuge, a royal or sacred fortress. Archaeologists are not sure who built Yagul or who is buried in its tombs, but most think it was the Mixtecs, who were the successors to the Zapotecs at Monte Albán.

The place was eerily empty. As we stood on a stone wall twice our height overlooking a rectangular courtyard of dry stubbled grass, four people approached along the top of the stonewall directly opposite us. Two had umbrellas—one black and one pink—others straw hats. An elderly women in a long black dress began to tell her companions about the ruins—was her accent British or Australian?—gesturing broadly with her arms over the empty expanse. I thought she must be archaeologist, so assured was her tone, though we could not hear the words. They seemed so contained in one another's company, their energy so bright against the stark, pale cobble of stone, that we just stood a moment and watched them as if they were a movie.

There was a big stone jaguar with a bowl cut into its back, once used in some ritual, now housed under a makeshift ramada. Narrow passages snaked through the Palace of the Six Patios, each patio surrounded by small sleeping quarters, labyrinthine corridors leading to more of the same. The place felt cramped, everything too close except the sky and distant vista. Each of us wandered separately for a while. We were unguided and glad for it, though no one said as much. I think something about the lonely quiet got into the bones of each of us. We were in a place built by people who had one place, and they answered to it with stones and blood and corn.

We drifted back together, glad again for casual company, and sat on the dead grass of the hilltop fortress watching red ants build a coarse, sandy mound and talking about the books that had mattered to us, the highlights of our respective travels and the range of our digestive woes. The conversation was idle and shifted like fair-weather clouds. Eventually the sun, climbing high and hot, began to get to us. We dusted off and headed downhill toward lunch. On the way out we encountered the caretaker, a young Mexican guy in blue chinos and white T-shirt.

We asked if he lived out here, and he said he did, in *la casa próx-ima*. And in the scrub we saw it, a tiny cement-block box where he stayed while tending the ruins. The thought of sleeping in the emptiness of the place was unsettling.

"Are there spirits here?" Josh asked, and it was what we all were thinking.

"Yes, a few," he answered. Later we got a laugh when Josh admitted that he had thought the man had said, "Yes, little ones."

"Sometimes they tap my shoulder or my chest when I'm sleeping," the caretaker continued. "They're benevolent spirits. I've seen the door open by itself. They sit beside me while I sleep."

Bent on celebrating our mutual ability to taste and digest, we hitched a ride to Teotitlán del Valle in the back of a farmer's pickup, breezing back down the highway through the grand emptiness of sun-parched hills. The side road to the village wound past prosperous brick houses, loose skeins of freshly died wool drying on the roofs—great looping bundles of earthy indigo, purple, forest green, rusty orange, turquoise and rose. The village streets were lined with shops and stalls selling brightly colored rugs depicting jaguar, serpent, parrot, Diego Rivera and Joan Miró motifs, and, most commonly, designs echoing the stone fretwork and idols of Mitla, Yagul and Monte Albán. The fretwork was apparent too in the village, if just barely so. Mexico is the land of "superimposed pasts," writes Paz.

> *Mexico City was built on the ruins of Tenochtitlán, the Aztec city that was built in the likeness of Tula, the Toltec city that was built in the likeness of Teotihuacán, the first great city on the American continent. Every Mexican bears*

within him this continuity, which goes back two thousand
years.

And so it was in Teotitlán, where the sixteenth-century
Catholic church had been built on top of Mitla-style ruins.
Those ruins were not much to see—a crumbling fretwork wall
sheltered by a reed ramada running a short block down a back
alley, impressively overshadowed by the turreted church and its
broad, copal-shaded courtyard. Unearthed only in recent years,
these ruins expose the missionary strategy of building on existing sacred ground. If a certain tree was held sacred because it
connected this world with the underworld, then the mission was
planted beside that tree. If the ruins of an ancient temple marked
a hilltop as sacred, that became the footprint for the new church.
In Mexican Catholicism it is not only the buildings that are layered onto an ancient, animistic substrate. There are villages, I
have been told, where animals are ritually sacrificed and, on the
day before the killing, are brought to church to be blessed. The
priest stays away from the sanctuary on that day, blessing the
act with his absence.

Cultural layering was everywhere in Teotitlán, where women
selling rugs to Bloomingdale's could be found gathered in a
backyard mixing a huge pot of atole with a medieval-looking
wooden paddle; where a teenager wearing a Beverly Hills T-shirt
would demonstrate the techniques for coaxing red and rose and
purple dyes from the cochineal parasite growing on prickly pear
cacti; where one could eat lunch at a restaurant well reviewed in
the *New York Times* and sit beside a woman on her knees grind-
ing corn on a metate—not on display for anyone, simply doing
her job—and be served lunch by another whose knee-length
hair was interbraided with traditional purple ribbons of cloth
and who would tell you that the magnificent weaving filling one

wall that depicted ancient deities had been made by her father, that it had taken him years, and he had built a special loom to make it.

We had arrived at La Casa de Abigail Mendoza just in time for the comida corrida and, casting caution to the pleasures of the moment, ordered mescal and chile soup and chicken cooked with mole negro or crusted with ground pumpkin seeds and basket after basket of fresh warm tortillas. We sipped the mescal from thimbles, dipping lime in rusty chile powder to balance the liquor's bite. The restaurant was in an atrium decked with huge vessels of gladioli and orange mums; strands of pastel paper cutouts garlanded the archways and unruly vines of philodendron sprawled up the white plaster walls. Through the arches was a dark colonnade where weavings hung from wall and rafters. I could have sat there for a week, watching the women transform carcasses, leaves, kernels and seeds into delicacies and sampling every one, first the molecules of scent swimming into my head, and then the flavors pooling in my mouth, and then the welcome dullness of satiety weighing the body down, no hunger at all calling it out of its satisfaction.

Of all the foods I loved in the Valley of Oaxaca, I loved none with more respect than mole negro. Its color and shine is that of gumtree sap, its flavor plays a chord that harmonizes fruity sweetness, *Capsicum* fire and bitter chocolate. It arouses so many zones of mouth, tongue and throat that the experience of a fine mole negro is erogenous. There are many stories about the origin of mole, just as there are many moles, some green, some red, some black. The word, from the Nahuatl *molli*, means simply "concoction." Diana Kennedy writes of the complex history of its unlikely marriage of ingredients. By her telling, all stories agree that mole was born in one of the convents in the city of Pueblo de los Angeles. The most respected version attributes the recipe to Sor Andrea, sister superior of the Santa Rosa convent, who wished to honor the visiting archbishop for his role in constructing her order's convent. She thought it would be fitting to blend new-world ingredients together with those of the old and so created mole poblano. Another story attributes mole to a visit by the viceroy Don Juan de Palafox y Mendoza, for which Fray Pascual was preparing a banquet at the convent. Turkeys were being cooked in *cazuelas* on the fire and, as Fray Pascual was scolding his assistants for their untidiness and sweeping their mess of spices onto a single tray, a sudden wind blew through the kitchen, spilling them into the *cazuelas*. Whether discovered by accident or intention, mole, as these stories attest, has a holy origin, is fit to honor the most distinguished guest, and celebrates the fruits of cross-cultural exchange. Perhaps a culture only rises to the level of civilization when its cuisine is refined and complex and delicious, when ingredients from far-flung regions marry into an integrated new whole. It is difficult to imagine a "civilization" that thrives on water and boiled potatoes, or on plastic pouches of Tang and reconstituted protein powder. "How civilized," we joke, sitting down to an elegant meal, a monument in fact to the civilization that has brought it to our table. For all of history's torment and brokenness, is there a better model for the peaceful crossing of borders than the history of food?

"For all its glory," wrote Robert Pogue Harrison in his luminous study of the history of forests, "civilization cannot console us for the loss of what it destroys. It destroys the matrix of its greatness, severing ancient bonds with the land on which the citizens build their monuments to power and civic heroism." At the table, however, where we celebrate the sacrifice of nature for civilization's advance, give thanks that we have transcended mere subsistence and the monotony of the locally grown, and share, if we are lucky, the warmth of good conversation, we may come as close as we can get to consolation.

At Abigail Mendoza's the conversation drifted to the economic history of Teotitlán. Among my companions, Jennie had been particularly interested to visit the village, having read *Zapotec Women*, Lynn Stephen's account of her anthropological work here. This was one of the most studied communities in Mexico, she said. It was months before I could get my hands on a copy of Stephen's work, but when I did that reading became fused with my experience in the place, two views in a stereopticon.

Indigenous women are the most marginalized sector of the Mexican population, Stephen writes. Their standard of living has progressed little or perhaps even declined since Cortés marched into Tenochtitlán in 1519. But while the state of Oaxaca has the lowest per capita gross product in Mexico, Teotitlán is prosperous both economically and ritually, thanks in large part to women's work. At the time of the Conquest, the Valley of Oaxaca was occupied by small city-states hostile to one another. The rise of Teotitlán probably resulted from the outflow of Zapotecs from Monte Albán, where as many as sixty thousand people lived a few centuries prior to its being abandoned by the year 700. Teotitlán, population now about five thousand, is still associated with pre-Conquest powers symbolized by a mountain called "brother rock" where ancient Teotitecos worshiped. The Zapotec name for the village means "under the rock." The place was also associated with a sun god who descended from the heavens as a bird. The ancient temple was built at the spot where this creature touched down. René Acuña's anthropological investigations say that early Teotitecos worshiped stone idols to which they offered their children in sacrifice. Today when

Catholic rituals are practiced during Holy Week, they are interrupted to perform rites urging rainfall and abundant crops. The village's July "Festival of Our Lord of the Precious Blood" draws people from throughout the region, as well as bringing back hundreds of locals now living in the United States.

Prior to the Conquest, Teotitecos wove with cotton on backstrap looms. Wool was introduced in the mid-sixteenth century by the first bishop to Oaxaca, who gave them sheep and taught them to card and spin wool and work on large treadle looms. By the mid-seventeenth century woolen blankets and serapes significantly fed the local economy. The community seems to have always had a strong sense of place, based on its fine weaving, elaborate ceremonial systems and unique spoken form of the Zapotec language. Teotitecos' institutions of *compadrazgo* and *guelaguetza* have traditionally earned households respect and authority in the community, as well as increasing the number of people an individual can count on as kin. *Compadrazgo* involves the sponsorship of unrelated godparents for important life-cycle ceremonies. Similar to elaborate sponsorship ceremonies that existed among the pre-Conquest Aztecs and Mayans, today it assists households to meet ritual obligations associated with the Catholic ceremonies of baptism, confirmation and marriage. *Guelaguetza* is a system of exchange that allows households to prepare in advance for "ceremonial consumption purposes." It consists of interest-free loans of goods, cash or labor made from one household to another over long periods of time. Loans are documented in notebooks (for those who can write) or memorized. Stephen offers this sample notebook from 1972:

Tereso Rodríguez	$100 (pesos)
Mario López	Six dozen eggs
Salvador Martínez	One turkey at 6 kilos

Francisco Pérez	2 kilos of cacao
Pedro Vicente	Three turkeys that together weigh 20 kilos
Manuel Pérez	2 almudes of beans
Luis Martínez	6 almudes of corn
Enrique Bautista	3 turkeys that together weigh 21.3 kilos
Manuel del Monte	10 1/2 almudes of tortillas (the amount of corn used)

And this narrative from a villager, aged fifty-two, named María.

I was married in 1953. My husband's mother paid for the ceremony. She actually didn't have to pay much money because she had inherited her mother's guelaguetzas. She was able to call in a lot of things that people owed her mother—turkeys, corn and cacao. She used these in the wedding. She could do this even though her mother was already dead. There were about fifty people at the wedding. We killed one pig and about twenty turkeys. I think the party went on for one or two days. There was no music and no dancing. The presents I got included a trunk, two metates, and about five or six blouses. . . . In 1968, my oldest daughter got married. It was a big party. There were about eighty couples invited and there was a band and dancing. She got two trunks, a dresser, and about eighteen different metates and some dishes. She got a lot more than I did. . . . My son was married in 1978. By then everyone had big weddings, not just the rich. There were 160 people at that wedding. There was music for two days and they killed three pigs. The bride got a trunk, a dresser, a glass case for her dishes, and lots of dishes. It was big wedding.

Young women, when invited to such a fiesta, work in teams fourteen hours a day making tortillas.

Teotitecos today continue to earn respect from participating in these traditions, though they must compete with merchants who earn respect for wealth acquired as exporters to Pier 1, Bloomingdale's and Filene's, as well as to European and Asian markets. Weavers and merchants alike take pride that Teotitecos were the originators of treadle loom weaving in the Oaxaca Valley. In terms of marketing their "authentic Zapotec weavings," it seems irrelevant to them that their methods and materials originally came from the Spanish. "Authentic Zapotec" seems to mean integrating outside influences. This is not a community that has defined itself by protective defense against outside influences.

A part of their story, as Stephen elaborates, is the Pan American Highway, completed in 1948 and linking the village with the larger Mexican economy. Another part is the 1940 Interamerican Indianist Congress held in Pátzcuaro, Michoacán, which marked the beginning of indigenist policy in Latin America. Prior to that the Department of Education and Culture for the Indian Race had been set up, and in 1927 the Casa del Estudiante Indigena to "eliminate the evolutionary distance that separates Indians from the present epoch, transforming their mentality, tendencies and customs . . . to incorporate them within the Mexican community." Programs taught agricultural and technological skills to the indigenous, but these did not reach some parts of Mexico until the 1940s. Even today in the mountains of Oaxaca there are small subsistence communities living in the forest with no desire to come out and participate in the contemporary economy. Teotitecos resisted these early efforts of the government to control local craft production and distribution. After the Indianist Congress, a systematic political, economic and social policy, with local implementation centers, was established to nationalize Mexico's more than fifty Indian groups. The centers promoted indigenous arts through expositions and competitions. Objects once made for use could now be made as arts and crafts, sold to "create ethnic identities" for Indians. Who was "Indian" was determined in the 1940s by asking, What language do you speak? Do you sleep on the floor or in a bed, on a mat or in a hammock? Do you wear shoes? Do you eat bread or tortillas? Those who spoke a Native language, slept on the floor or in a hammock, went barefoot and ate tortillas were "Indians."

This policy continued into the 1950s, when the Mexican government looked to tourism as a way to bring money into poor indigenous communities, which were encouraged "to maintain and reproduce certain outwardly picturesque characteristics— in particular, dress, ritual, and craft production, which make them identifiable as Indians to tourists." Thus several decades of government policy helped to create "the official Mexican Indian." The Teotitecos' strong sense of identity kept them somewhat aloof from these initiatives. Their continued self-definition helped other ethnolinguistic groups in the valley to resist being homogenized into one "Indian" identity.

Yet another part of their story is World War II. The U.S. labor shortage during the war led the United States and Mexico to collaborate in bringing workers to the North with governmental protection of their rights. So sensitive were both governments to workers' rights that migrants were not sent to Texas because of its history of discrimination against Mexicans. Men who had been subsistence farmers at home began to work for a wage. They were taken to Mexico City, given a haircut, clothes and shoes, and sent to work. After the war, migrant workers' rights were no longer protected, but that did not stop them from crossing the border for jobs. Some came home and bought land with their earnings. Many continued the pattern of seasonal migration. With the men gone, women had to work the fields, gather firewood, haul water, do the spinning and weaving, and care for children. Everyone who remained at home worked hard beginning at age five or six. They were very poor, having one set of clothes that they washed at the river, waiting there for them to dry. In the 1970s women too began to migrate to work as housekeepers and nannies, or to pick strawberries in California for a dollar a box, running to hide in garbage cans when the *migra* patrolled. There was no water in the fields, except what was there for the produce. They learned to eat tomatoes for the water.

By the 1980s, surveys of the village found that from 25 to 50 percent of households had men working in the United States; in many cases two generations of men were missing. The women who stayed at home became very independent; often they were sole wage earners. Sometimes the men sent money home and sometimes they did not. Some had children by several women and sent money to one and not to others. Some men never came back, leaving women to raise young children on their own. During this same period—the 1970s and 1980s—the U.S. market demand for weavings increased, and women began in large numbers to practice what had been largely a male occupation. The town's independence began to pay off as they developed market relationships with U.S. importers without government middlemen interceding and taking a cut.

As the international market boomed, a new class of merchants emerged in Teotitlán, and though they were resented for getting rich "without doing the work," they earned respect by being better able to participate in *compadrazgo* and *guelaguetza*. Poorer women could still use ritual to earn respect, while many of the younger ones—often literate and bilingual—earned respect for their knowledge and wealth. It was the women, by and large, who kept these ritual institutions alive. As part of the government's promotion of indigenous life as a tourist attraction, the village performed celebrations of saints' days in the public plaza, the same place used for such national holidays as Mexican Independence Day, Mother's Day and the Day of the Revolution—all open to outsiders. In households, by nature protected from tourists, Teotitecos engage in the more private rituals of kinship and exchange, reshuffling some of the inequities that have developed with the town's prosperity. Every day in the village has become a complex web of allegiances and oppositions. Merchants may use outstanding kinship loans to recruit their godchildren as pieceworkers; weavers may choose not to complete a large order placed by an American client because they are cooking for the baptism of their compadres' son. The new authority of wealth competes with the old authority of kinship. Villagers take pride in high levels of ritual consumption and "readily admit that occasions such as weddings have turned into contests of one-upmanship," Stephen writes.

> *The amount of food and candles given at local engagement ceremonies is now so great that gifts have to be transported on a flatbed truck from the house of the prospective groom to the house of his future bride. . . . While some younger sectors of the community, particularly merchants, say that they want to stop spending so much time and money on fiestas, they acknowledge that social pressure to maintain* costumbre *(custom) is very strong.*

Unluckily, the vicissitudes of my illness made it impossible for me to keep up with my cooking class at the institute. I had been present for the murky business of atole, though preparing this drink was a skill I could not imagine employing. I had learned to identify hierba santa *(Piper sanctum)*, large heart-shaped leaves that imparted, as did lightly toasted avocado leaves, the anise flavor to beans or sauces. And I had nested masa into cradles of corn husk, tying them closed with narrow strands of the same vegetable membrane, to prepare tamales for steaming. But I had missed the real test of culinary finesse, making mole negro from scratch. I later copied down the recipe, hopeful that I could translate it accurately enough to make the sauce on my own. I had already learned that our cooking teacher used written recipes only as an approximation of a process she knew too well to pin down. *"Sí, sí, dos cucharas,"* she'd reply when asked to clarify a detail, and then she'd grab a loose handful of the stuff to demonstrate.

Learning to cook is like learning to dance. You cannot master the tango by placing your feet in footsteps drawn on the floor. I knew I was merely copying down such footsteps. The recipe listed twenty-two ingredients, including four different chiles: chilhuacles, mulatos, pasillas, chipotles. It called for banana, raisins, chunks of egg bread, almonds, peanuts, walnuts, sesame seeds, onion, cloves, sugar, oregano, thyme, marjoram, cinnamon, garlic, tomatoes, tomatillos and a thick bar of dark Oaxacan chocolate. It began with toasting the chiles over flame and ended with pouring the sauce over pieces of chicken cooked in garlic and onion.

I did not get to try out my dance steps until a few weeks later, while visiting friends in Todos Santos on the west coast of Baja California Sur, where I had access to a kitchen and the good graces of their willingness to be my guinea pigs. David and Phyllis Burks are migratory animals who spend their summers in Oregon and winters on the Baja Peninsula. They have a little house and guest casita surrounded by papaya, banana, grapefruit and pomegranate trees. The place is loaded with birds—hooded orioles, flickers, and Xantus hummingbirds (green with cinnamon tail, white eye stripe, and red bill). These creatures, I suspected, must have given my friends the idea that living in two locations might be better than one. I felt a little sorry for myself by the time I got there, missing Oaxaca, resenting how much this town had conceded to tourists from the North: signs and menus and prices tailored for recreational vehicles and tour buses making the Baja run to Cabo; street vendors chased away by shopkeepers bent on keeping the third world off their doorsteps; the home of Don Henley's "Hotel California" (a song the town will never let rest), once a counterculture collective slung with hammocks for people who wanted to check out, now a neo-funky tour site for high-paying customers who want to check in; a town that happily takes the spillover of California surfer culture—bumper stickers from Bodega Bay and Huntington Beach plastered on surfboards and VW buses, and more tie-dye and patchouli oil than I have seen and smelled for thirty years.

But the back streets were consoling, dirty and quiet and neighborly. I walked them for days, photographing wattle-and-daub houses with fan palm roofs, drawing mahogany banana flowers, and marveling at the geometry of newly cut furrows with their weft of acequias. And when the day approached on which David and Phyllis would be busy selling their carvings and prints at a craft fair, I volunteered to make dinner, thinking that to revel in the intricacies of mole would surely lift me from the funk of feeling displaced. We spent a day shopping in La Paz. I tried the *mercado municipal* for chiles. The pasillas and mulatos were not a problem. Great mounds of them filled bins and baskets. As for the chipotles, several merchants offered me a canned version. No, no, I insisted, I need the fresh ones, picturing the shriveled brown things I had seen in Oaxaca. But when I asked for chilhuacles negros, vendors drew a blank. They suggested I go around the corner to the Semilla de Guadalajara. There I showed the vendor the recipe to make sure I had the words right. Having missed the mole class, I did not know what I was looking for and could not describe the missing link, only that it was indispensable to mole oaxaqueño. No luck. I settled for some robust guajillos and a few anchos, though I had no idea what flavor they would impart. For a chipotle surrogate, I settled on tiny moritas which seemed smoky enough to pass. I fared even worse looking for hierba santa for flavoring the black beans. Two women suggested I visit Doña Christina's medicinal plant shop. A man there took out a plant encyclopedia bearing Latin and popular names. We found an illustration bearing that name, but the leaf was nothing like the big hearts I had seen farther south. I resigned myself to tossing a few moritas in the kettle with the beans and hoping for the best.

I had the day alone in the house to fill the kitchen with chaotic industry, to let simple ingredients slowly marry into something complex, carrying me back through my journey and into the present. I thought how strange it was that both the most rudimentary and the most sophisticated cuisines relied upon the handmade. I thought of all the hands that had made the meal possible. The merchants who advised and weighed and bagged and passed me change, the farmers who hewed and coaxed the land to produce, the ditchmen who made the water flow by gravity to the chile fields, the bugs and birds and bats who helped the sexual work of plants so they could bear, the miners who dug the ore and smelters who turned it to steel for the pots I cooked in, the ancient ones who saw and tasted weeds and taught them to be more exuberant, the priests who taught people to pray and praise when they feared for their lives and their crops, the earth, the earth, the blessed earth that holds us on its back without a shrug and will take us in one day and all our inventions as it takes in every kind of fodder and makes it into something else.

Outside the flickers and flycatchers scrapped over what was left of the ripening bananas. The sounds of raking in gravel, sweeping on pavement, a truck Dopplering past, filtered into the house. The sunlight, screened through the broad banana leaves, took on a soft lime green shine. The mole cooked, and it was sweet and hot and dark as a colonial convent. Wattle and daub, wattle and daub, I kept picturing those structures built from what was on hand: the slender pliable branches bent and woven to make walls, wads of clay filling in the cracks, overlapping fronds for the roof—a shelter built of dirt and sticks, the kind of house we dream of making as children when we built forts of blankets and chairs, or pine boughs and scrap lumber, the kind of shelter that is never as secure as we dream it will be.

chapter 8

Return

This thing we call "civilization"—all these physical and moral comforts, all these conveniences, all these shelters, all these virtues and disciplines which have become habit now, on which we count, and which in effect constitute a repertory or system of securities which man made for himself like a raft in the initial shipwreck which living always is—all these securities are insecure securities which in the twinkling of an eye, at the least carelessness, escape from man's hands and vanish like phantoms. History tells us of innumerable retrogressions, of decadences and degenerations. But nothing tells us that there is no possibility of much more basic retrogressions than any so far known, including the most basic of them all: the total disappearance of man as man and his silent return to the animal scale, to complete and definitive absorption in the other.

—José Ortega y Gasset

I had my doubts about the walk past a ruined sugar mill down a narrow dirt road into the broad arroyo separating Todos Santos from the Pacific, but I felt cramped in town, the sun kept staring me in the face, and the trail kept opening in front of me. "Just keep heading west," my friends had chirped, and so I took my fear of rattlesnakes, scorpions, mad dogs, drug dealers and rapists out for a pastoral afternoon stroll. Fear is not such a bad companion to take on an outing into nature. It makes one not a mere spectator, but a participant, subject to the random cruelties of the animal world, alert to the entire surround. I suspect most field biologists get a buzz from this sensation, though they may focus their attention on collecting flower and leaf samples of endangered plants, picking apart scat for the dietary story it will tell, or gathering fur caught in a bramble to take to the lab for DNA analysis. I assume that just being out in a part of the world not dominated by human invention makes one's senses revert to an animal acuity—a physical response to a physical world that we experience metaphysically.

This village was once the sugarcane capital of the Baja Peninsula, with five thriving mills. By 1950, after the freshwater spring feeding the arroyo dried up, the industry was all but gone. The last mill closed in 1965. Fifteen years later the spring came back, and the arroyo again was tilled, this time producing avocados, mangoes, coconuts, papayas, corn, beans and chiles. It is an unlikely sight, this lush and fertile oasis running a few miles long and deep on the arid peninsula's edge. Hills rise back from the village looking gray and severe, spotted with *pitaya agria*, chain-link cholla, creosote bush and *cardón* cactus. Cattle with ribs as thin as wattle free-range over the thorny desert.

I set out down the dirt track past the tumbling brick walls of the mill, winding downhill into sugarcane and brushy trees that canopied the road. A scrappy corral built with branches, many no thicker than my forefinger, sheltered a well-groomed bay pony. Thickets of purple-stemmed castor bean towered into the trees. A foot-wide cement canal carried chalky water along the roadside. Narrow sluiceways were hoed into the ground, opened or closed with a spadeful of dirt and weeds to channel the gravity flow into the fields. The thirsty brown dirt was stained where it had drunk, furrows trenched into the fields so that every row was soaked, though not a metal pipe, pump or tractor was in sight. The arroyo was a quilt of wild and cultivated patches, and the farther I wandered into it, from dirt road to foot track to the meander through scorched fan palms and coconuts, the more I admired this collaboration between people and plants and water. Irregular plots of perfectly geometrical furrows were cut between rangy thickets of vegetation. There was no walking in a straight line toward the beach. The plots had been laid out in a way that made sense for those working the land, not those bustling through it. The ocean that lay a few miles beyond was too cold and violent for beach culture to have taken it over. It was merely beautiful, and a little hard to get to, so the tourists didn't bother much with it. I made my jagged way along a field here, through a fence stile there, up a lane here, down a wooded foot path there, and on, trying to make the turns average out to "Just keep heading west."

I met a stocky gray-haired man from Las Vegas who was pulling onto a lane barely wide enough for his pickup truck. He said he'd taken a year off and rented a house in the arroyo. A clutch of rusty hens picked around in his dirt yard. He'd been here for six months and said he liked to take pictures of birds down at the lagoon—egrets and herons. But he didn't like the filth. "I had to pick up a lot of garbage before I could get a decent picture." What had he left behind, I wondered, to need this quiet life? I passed a man hoeing, another wrestling with a single-horse plow, a couple of men leaning on trees in the shade, machetes belted at their sides, another leading a finely muscled horse on a rope halter (he asked me to take a picture and sweet-talked her into posing). All were cordial and urged me on, pointing toward the westering sun, though the machetes, I confess, nearly turned me around. I trusted, perhaps stupidly, the magic of small talk to diffuse hostility. "These fields are beautiful, aren't they?" I would offer. "What crop is this you are growing? Is it difficult to grow it here?" I was less afraid chatting with machete-wielding campesinos in the middle of nowhere than I would have been on most urban streets. My sense of risk began to subside as the day's beauty rose.

The last patch in the quilt, before sand dunes gave out to the beach, was a scorched stand of tended fan and coconut palms. Wind rustled the stiff fronds in big gusts, the sound thick and dry, and flickers knocked their heads against the trunks for bugs. In a small grove that I mistook for wild, cut fronds had been laid on the ground to dry, then wrapped and tied into spiraling bales that stood on end. The symmetry of those bundles, the compression that had turned the singular flat fronds into fat torchy bouquets, the way they all stood up together in the center of the clearing as if ready to take a bow, made me think I had stumbled onto an art project—a masterwork by Andy Goldsworthy, the sculptor who rearranges what he finds in the woods until it turns into art. Then I remembered the leafy palapas that covered patios, restaurant ramadas and shacks all over town, and I knew this was work, not art, though the difference was indistinguishable. Someone had just harvested a roof.

Pericú and Guaycura Indians once inhabited the Baja Peninsula, living nomadically and harvesting small game, wild plants and shellfish. When the Spanish came in the sixteenth century, they found people along the coast wearing pearls. This sign of beauty to the indigenous was a sign of wealth to the newcomers, who began their own harvesting from the sea. La Paz, the first European settlement on the peninsula, became a great pearl center, until oyster stocks became depleted. Religion followed. In

Todos Santos the first Jesuit mission was built in 1733, then destroyed in the capewide Indian revolt of 1734. The padres who were not killed fled east to Isla del Espíritu Santo. An army of Spanish soldiers and their Yaqui converts was sent to retaliate. The rebels were executed and the church rebuilt. Finally, it was not commerce or religion that changed the complexion of the region but smallpox, which struck the Baja Indians with gruesome force. In Todos Santos their population went from 700 in 1768 to 181 in 1800. In 1849 the mission was closed for lack of worshipers.

I made it to the beach, where I found not a soul for miles. In the distance rose the headland of Punta Lobos, where fishermen were launching boats into the surf to search for sierra and huachinango. Flocks of pelicans skimmed the sand near the tideline, eyes fixed on the water, rising a dozen feet to increase their distance as they passed me. The surf hammered the white beach, waves rising taller than the little houses in town, scouring the sand like bulldozers. In one span of vision I saw the riled-up Pacific, blades of sun piercing through the pure blue sky, the lip of white sand that ran a hundred miles along the coast, and miles of unpeopled desert rising to the stark ridgeline of the Sierra de la Laguna. A few isolated palms poked up from oases. How contingent life is in the desert, how transforming the rush of inland water in a channel opened by the turning of a spade, the flow rolling into fields, and bleeding into cellular tissues, pooling and mixing there, and catalyzing the necessary change to keep life going.

My stay in the village came near the end of an extended ramble in Mexico, and as the time to return home approached, I grew more greedy for experiences of culture I would not be able to have at home. They were not hard to find. One afternoon while I lounged in my friends' patio observing the courtship ritual between a hummingbird and a banana flower, Jesús, the care-taker, arrived to rebuild the rotting palapa over my head. I watched him sort the dried palm fronds from a heap, then hose them down so the nails wouldn't split the stalks when he hammered them in place. In my backyard in Tucson I had a couple of fan palms, and I thought it would not hurt to learn how to use the spiny fronds I regularly trimmed from their trunks.

"How long do you have to dry them?" I asked.

"You can cut them dry and use them right away," Jesús explained, "but if you cut them green, let them dry for three or four days. And cut them with the full moon—if you cut them at the quarter moon, they'll fall apart. When they cut them for money they don't pay any attention to that, but it's very important."

Jesús had no teeth. He'd lost them drunk in a fight. Since then he had given up drinking. I had seen only his gentle side—his tending of the papaya and banana orchard, his building of lovely cement berms, textured with a trowel to look like ropy lava, for channeling rainwater, and his disdain for the rotten condition of the palapa that would no longer hold back the rain. It was hard to picture him reeling and bloody from another man's fists.

He separated the good fronds from the bad, setting loose spiders, cockroaches and two glassine scorpions. The latter were bleached-looking, as if they had lived in the dark all their lives and learned to create their own dull light. Their stingers were curled upwards over their backs, little knapsacks of poison. I shrank back as Jesús poked them apart from the heap.

"They won't kill you. They just make a big sore," he said gesturing to his forearm, "but it only lasts a day." He held one with a stick and cut its stinger off, then raised it up in his palm to show me how harmless it was.

"They eat a lot of insects," he said, appreciative, and set it loose.

"I've seen scorpions six inches long," he said, squashing a black widow in his palm, "but the smaller ones make you sicker." Jesús cannot read or write, and I do not know if that is a source of regret for him. But it is a source of honor that through working he has learned this place by touch, right down to its venom.

Another day I set off with my hosts in their Jeep over the washboard sand roads to explore the hill towns, once rich from mining, now leached out and uncertain about their future. In the mid-1800s the residents of El Triunfo had been taking fifty thousand dollars' worth of gold and silver daily from their hills. Now a few streetside stands sold straw baskets and iguanas, and one shirt-making *maquiladora* gave a few dozen people work. We stopped in San Antonio for lunch, a town that seemed better off than many, since it had a convent, a dairy and what appeared to be a local cable TV company (a satellite dish corralled inside a chain-link fence). After a picnic in the shady plaza, we each set off separately to explore. I found, on the outskirts of town, a path lined with whitewashed stones that led up a steep hill to a small shrine overlooking the village. It looked like a hot, hard walk, but the path was trodden and worn. Before I got close enough to decide whether I had the stamina for the pilgrimage, I was stopped in my tracks by something closer. On the side of the dirt road sprawled a broad mesquite tree and from its lowest bough, still well above my head, swung a lynched cat. It was a gray tiger with white mask and belly, and its body had begun to cave in and stink with rot. It was only a small violence, yet someone had had the premeditated desire to kill, to display the killing as an act of vengeful justice, and to leave the body hanging and filling the public air with its putrescence. The cruelty was boastful, a vision enacted, its malevolence leaking all over town. As if on cue, a pickup approached and slowed. Three men in the cab looked me over, looked at each other, slowed some more.

"*Hola,*" they said. "*Hola,*" I said, but the small talk now seemed to hold no protective magic. Another truck came up from behind them and honked, and the lurkers sped off.

Before leaving Todos Santos, I paid my respects to the dead at the village cemetery, a bright, familial gated community, cluttered with plastic and Kleenex flowers stuck in Pepsi cans and Clorox bottles, crypts topped with hanging Christ, kneeling angel, cement or plywood cross. The oldest graves were collapsing brick mausoleums, the plaster long eroded off, Grecian urns topping the corners. On the roof of one, a vagrant barrel cactus had rooted. Behind each gravesite, whether grand or small, was a *nichito* built of clay or brick or tin for burning candles. These were littered with blackened matches and squares of foil left to shelter the flame from wind, the chambers stained with the thick soot of prayers. Even the poorest and oldest graves, dating to the mid-1800s, were not forgotten: a mound of earth with a weathered plywood cross leaning against a fence post wore a fresh garland of Kleenex carnations protectively covered with Saran Wrap. The soil was little more than desert dust; most burials were shallow and covered with a cement slab, some painted heavenly blue. Many bore no inscriptions. One had a foot-square cement monument tiled on all four sides with chips of crockery—blue willowware dinner plate, the cheek of a Little Bo Peep teacup, a saucer ringed with pansies, plates striped and solid—shards of a treasured, broken domesticity.

While I wandered over the spare threads of weed and grass, a man entered the gate pushing a wheelbarrow full of cement bags and bricks. He chattered to the teenage boy and toddler who accompanied him, and the sound of conversation was welcome and strange in that quiet place. They wheeled up midway into the cemetery where a hose led from a cistern to a faucet, and they set to work mixing mortar. The man and the teenager talked idly, as men do when they work, bubbles of conversation rising, until the toddler began to cry. The teenager—perhaps the kid's older brother—went to him, his voice arcing into gentle questions. Then he led the boy into the shade of a crypt, wet a rag, slid off the boy's soiled pants, cleaned him, then rinsed the underpants in the hose, the teenager's voice all the while cooing comfort to the little one, and the water that would not shut off dripping and dripping into a cluster of lilies growing around the trunk of a small dead tree.

On the way home, I flew from La Paz to Guaymas to meet ethnobotanist Gary Nabhan, who was on his way to Seri country on the west coast of Sonora. There we traveled and camped for a week with a small group of students, visiting the local residents, gathering stories and trading them for tools, clothes, crayons, notebooks, pens and vitamins. We learned about buck deer on Isla Tiburón that don't rut or breed or lose the velvet on their antlers. They grow very large and have the finest meat, the most prized by hunters, while the meat from animals expending their energy in courtship and mating tastes disgusting. We learned about a biologist who came to spend a few months on the island. He said he knew all about the desert and didn't want a guide. The Seris tried to change his mind, but he refused. Later they found his remains with a note he'd written explaining that he'd been bitten by a snake, had used antivenin and plants, but nothing had worked. We learned about a Seri man who thinks he is a woman and leads a deer all around the island on a rope. We learned that February is the month when millions of small sea animals migrate, March when the big sea creatures migrate, April when the eel grass first sprouts, May when people build ramadas and are happy, June the month when there are lots of fruits for making wine. We learned about a man hunting on the island who met a spirit that told him, "I'm going to shoot you through with lead. If you let me do it, you will have great powers and live to be old. If not, you'll die." He let himself be shot and lived to be an old man. When he came back to the village, someone tried to care for his wound, but he said no. We learned about a man who had died of hunger, a respected elder who had given a great deal of information to visiting researchers. "He made it possible," the guide said, "for them to write their books. Why didn't they help him when he was starving?"

We gave away as much stuff as we could think of, even the hats off our heads, and bought necklaces and baskets and ironwood carvings. Our last night in Mexico before driving home, we camped in a disjunct population of boojum trees south of Libertad. They are the only wild boojums outside of their native habitat on the Baja Peninsula, and we planted ourselves among those exotics that look like upturned roots making a halfhearted attempt to produce leaves. Gary was concerned for their future, because an invasive wild mustard was spreading toward them, a weed that makes the sand dunes more susceptible to fire. I was grateful that his knowledge helped me see more than their odd beauty, though tired, very tired, of the news that another way of life was threatened.

That night whatever hostile intestinal microbes I had collected over many weeks of traveling in Mexico rallied once again. I suspected the fish tacos in Todos Santos had reinoculated me, or the filth of the villages where we had sat on the ground sharing stories while mangy dogs and chickens scrambled beside us. I wondered if the microvermin would plant me permanently under this desiccated soil, my final contribution to the world to feed the last of an outcast tribe of boojums. My system exploded at intervals all night, and I staggered again and again out of a

sleeping-bag fever to dig a divot in the hard soil in which to re-
lieve myself. I took minor consolation that I was traveling with
a friend dear enough and articulate enough to make a good story
of my death.

But one sunrise, a dozen saltines, and two bottles of ginger ale
later, we crossed the border at Nogales, and I began to rejoin the
ribald joking that a certain member of our party was prone to
fostering.

"What would you say in a moment of passion to a man
named Ponderosa?"

"PON-der-O-sa!" someone sang out.

"This is the best of the old growth for me," said another mod-
estly.

"Talk about a tall timber . . ."

"Take a bough!"

"TIM-BER!"

"You sure can recover quickly after a fire."

Dusk crept in as we headed for Tucson, the desert stark and
glowing electric rose, a hill here or there forming a black sil-
houette against the sky as we zipped along the highway. Soon the
lights of settlement began to appear, first in cozy clusters, then in
twinkling yellow strings and grids, then sprawling out forever,
leaking into the sky and eating up the dark. A huge red Arby's
sign shone circus-bright, then Taco Bell and Texaco and Circle K,
each with colors and shapes that identified them like didactic il-
lustrations in a children's book. I could stop anywhere, I thought
with relief, and drink the water freely. I was back in the big, clean,
glittering, corporate U.S.A. and grateful to be home.

One day while I idled in traffic waiting for a light to change, the
massive sheet-metal wall of a Jeep Cherokee idling next to me

and dwarfing my rent-a-wreck Nissan, I was struck with the notion of how unlikely all of this is: that an animal should drive cars, should know how to build them, how to build roads, and to make them go everywhere on earth; that an organism should invent electricity and engines and dig metal out of the earth so it could ride it to the moon; that an animal should remember during the day the bright face of the moon at night and that the feeling induced by its beauty could come equally from the moon's presence and from the memory of the moon; that a creature should make laws its conspecifics would obey, if they felt they were good and necessary laws; that an animal should know what "good" and "necessary" mean, and that their meanings could change in different contexts; that it should think up money and justice and beauty and war as if these were things that had always existed, like rocks and stars and space; that an animal should know that "always" means only "since the beginning of time," an event it understands as spatial, "the Big Bang."

There is no story more interesting to me than that of the evolution of the human mind. Short version: Four million years ago a human-ape named *Australopithecus afarensis* (the Lucy species) climbed out of the African trees, walked on two feet and began to carry things in his arms for long distances. Two million years ago little bands of handymen, *Homo habilis*, one of three contemporary species of hominids, foraged for a living and used flaked stone tools, speaking the language of two-year-olds to describe the location of food or announce danger. Their brain volume was half that of modern humans, though they were recognizable as human, marking the evolutionary crossing from animal to us. The final steps by which that ancestor evolved into *Homo erectus*, who by 350,000 years ago knew the use of fire and ocher pigments, and then *Homo sapiens*, who has been around for only 100,000 years or so, mark the fastest and most complex growth spurt in the history of life. Nature had developed a prodigy.

Australopithecus laid the groundwork with upright posture and bipedalism, freeing hands to carry animal prey, tubers and fruits long distances back to the campsite. This led to the sharing of food, which led to kinship groups in which communication and cooperation developed, improving the odds that a creature without big teeth and claws could compete successfully for food. Thus from very early on, our ancestors learned to get what they needed from the environment by enhancing their physical capabilities with cultural learning. Long-term memory and language, made possible by the large primate brain, sped up the process.

Charles J. Lumsden and Edward O. Wilson have described its mechanism in *Promethean Fire: Reflections on the Origin of Mind:*

> *Somehow the evolving species kindled a Promethean fire, a self-sustaining reaction that carried humanity beyond the previous limits of biology. This largely unknown evolutionary process we have called gene-culture coevolution: it is a complicated, fascinating interaction in which culture is generated and shaped by biological imperatives while biological traits are simultaneously altered by genetic evolution in response to cultural innovation. We believe that gene-culture coevolution, alone and unaided, has created man and that the manner in which the mechanism works can be solved by a combination of techniques from the natural and social sciences.*

During the four million formative years, weather in Africa alternated between ice age and warmer conditions in regular cycles shifting every forty thousand years or so (the intervals changed, but the overall pattern persisted). Our ancestors were the strand of hominids that learned to adapt to this unpredictable world. Among their strategies was traveling to distant regions as climatic conditions shifted. Other hominid strains did not fare as well. The Neanderthals ranged over a more limited area and became extinct, though we still claim kinship with them because they buried their dead with flowers. By twenty-five thousand years ago, Cro-Magnons left evidence of the growing legacy of mind, painting the interior walls of caves with images of creatures that occupied their inner lives. And so the human-made world began. After another twenty thousand years, city-states began to inscribe Earth with the pattern of our civilization— complex economies, social hierarchies, refinements in art, science and religion and written systems (beginning in the Middle East with a system of cones, spheres and triangles pressed into clay) to keep track of it all. Among our oldest and most formative habits are walking around, sharing food and learning, and making art.

This is our story, as we best understand it at this time.

Where are we now in the human story? That is what I have been trying to get at in my travels and speculation. We are the first people to see ourselves as participating in a story four million years old, and the first to contemplate our evolutionary destiny. What we see is this: five thousand years of city-states at first discrete, then spilling into one another with violence and confusion as political boundaries had to be redefined; five hundred years of becoming global, beginning with the voyages of discovery and ending with the Internet, the electronic lace stitching the world together into one fabric woven of little neotribal communities based on informational affinity; one hundred years of dazzling technology and science that have changed for the better our relationship with nature, time, place, work, suffering and death; fifty years of intoxicating material invention—the Bomb, the Pill, footprints on the moon, fingerprints on genes, instruments expanding our vision farther into space than our minds can comprehend, the brand-new fusing of microchip and DNA technologies that makes actual the sci-fi dream of cyborgs; and a few decades of the sobering global perspective that while our species has been sprawling clumsily across the planet trying to figure out how to get along with itself, it has (both willfully and accidentally) torn the fabric of nature into tattered islands where extinction is occurring, according to E. O. Wilson, "thousands of times faster than the production of new species." This last is a fact not incidental, but central, to our story. "The human species," Wilson asserts, "is an environmental hazard."

I have clipped a ghoulish photograph from a *New York Times Magazine* special issue on technology. A middle-aged man sits on a steel laboratory stool. Behind him stands a bank of monitors, oscilloscopes, dials, switches, surgical lamps and IV poles hung with sacks of saline or glucose solution. The man is well dressed in an expensive, California way—pale rose Oxford-cloth shirt buttoned at the neck, tawny worsted trousers crisply pressed. He is a large man, his face dull and pasty, lips thin and unsmiling, eyes set into shadowy recesses, forehead high and square—he looks a lot like Frankenstein. But the photo is no joke or fiction (though I suspect the photographer worked the angles and lighting to enhance this similarity). Beside the man sits a robust German shepherd, leashed, both man and dog looking right into the camera's lens, the man's hand comforting on the dog's head, or perhaps gently holding the collar to sustain the pose.

The man is Saul Kent, cofounder of the Life Extension Foundation in Southern California, where he and his staff have been experimenting with cryonic freezing as an alternative to death. He has brought his pet dog, Franklin, to within a few degrees above freezing and successfully revived him after five hours of "having essentially no normal blood circulation to the brain." Dozens of other dogs have died in his experiments. The problem is that freezing creates expanding ice crystals that rupture cells and organs. "Kent became a fringe celebrity," the article elaborates, "after the 1987 death of his mother, Dora Kent, who had signed up for cryonic preservation as a 'neuro' (head-only) patient. (Many cryonics advocates believe that science will one day be able to grow a new body around a preserved brain.)" This is the ultimate anthropocentrism, a perspective Wilson defines. "To be anthropocentric is to remain unaware of the limits of human nature, the significance of biological processes underlying human behavior, and the deeper meaning of long-term genetic evolution."

Kent's version of the future is one in which we leave nature behind for a completely human-made world, and it rhymes with the version that says we will colonize space in time to escape the mess we have made of Earth. Both of these versions believe that human beings are smart enough, or will be soon, to take over the controls from nature and steer it where we want it to go. They follow the trajectory set in the past few centuries of our increasing exemption from nature's rules. Any exemptions we have earned, however, are extremely limited. One example, taken for granted but nevertheless profound, is our control of human reproductive technology. Enhanced sexuality, the evolutionary theorists tell us, is very ancient in us, part of the hominid success story. It goes something like this: Female hominid gives male no biological signal when she is in estrus. The other primates are more physically communicative about the matter, raising a rosy rump, so to speak, when an egg is ready for sperm. Rather than being discouraged by the female hominid's discretion, the male reads that she is available for sex all the time, and her pleasure in the act, along with his, confirms this reading. This arouses him further and makes him stick around and, incidentally, help to raise the young. He gets easy sex, she gets help with the kids. The species becomes a big success because of this contract, based upon a misunderstanding that women have been trying to correct ever since. Given a hundred thousand years or so of that history, it should not surprise us that now, even though we have managed to control the reproductive aspect of our sexual behavior, we are still befuddled about who wants what, when, on what terms, and what we *ought* to want. We have learned to control one particular mechanism of human sexuality, but the whole matrix within which that mechanism functions is not only beyond our control but beyond our understanding. Cloning, the next step in the control of reproductive technology, is stirring up new anxieties about the moral uses of human power. So far, no one really wants to go back in technological time on reproductive matters. This kind of control of nature is as welcome to us as are oil furnaces, air conditioners, immunizations, antibiotics and cardiac defibrillators. But as one example of how limited our control actually is, this story reminds us that we may not yet be quite capable of leaving nature behind.

One may be tempted to blame science for the natureless vision of the future, for to contemplate Saul Kent working in his laboratory beside the frozen, severed head of his mother is to conjure up the popular image of the Mad Scientist. But the cryonic vision is based upon materialism, not science. Science tells us that death is necessary, that each individual life contributes incrementally to the work-in-progress that is the life of Life. To overcome individual death would be to violate the very core of the biological principle by which we exist at all. Because our evolutionary predecessors lived and died, we live and die. We cannot possibly conceive what our distant successors—*Homo animus?* insects? bacteria? "biomechanoids"?—will make of our legacy. Surely the extended life span we enjoy in this century is one of science's most precious gifts to us. Nevertheless, when the time comes, we step aside, as our successors will step aside, making room for the gene pool to diversify so that the process of evolution will continue for as long as conditions on Earth support life. There are limits to our power over matter. They are limits set by nature, and one of them is death.

The other version of the future is loud with grief and warning, because its proponents, myself among them, see human beings as more deeply embedded in nature than we have been able to appreciate until now. This view is rooted in the knowledge that contemporary science gives us about our past, about the complex interdependencies among species, and about the price other species have been made to pay for our comforts. Wilson writes that it will take millions of years to correct the loss of genetic and species diversity caused by our destruction of natural habitats; and, further, that "humanity is now destroying most of the habitats where evolution can occur." It may be difficult to anticipate what actions deemed good in the present will appear in the future to be unjust, even unforgivable. Both the Aztec practice of human sacrifice and the Spanish zeal to replace it with Catholicism, for example, appear to us to be morally repugnant. Which of our practices will our descendants find difficult to forgive? Surely it will be our heartless, greed-driven slaughter of nature.

These days I think that the people who feel pain when they witness the wounded condition of Earth feel that the wounding is taking place in themselves. Our ideas about the material world are no longer material and mechanical: objects interacting with other discrete objects as in a medieval orrery. Matter is now understood to be a pattern of events, a field of reactions, a continuous flow. Biophysicist Harold Morowitz has written about how this understanding informs our experience of the natural environment:

> Viewed from the point of view of modern [ecology], each living thing is a dissipative structure, that is, it does not endure in and of itself but only as a result of the continual flow of energy in the system. . . . From this point of view, the reality of individuals is problematic because they do not exist per se but only as local perturbations in this universal energy flow. . . . An example might be instructive. Consider a vortex in a stream of flowing water. The vortex is a structure made of an ever-changing group of water molecules. It does not exist as an entity in the classical Western sense; it exists only because of the flow of water through the stream. If the flow ceases the vortex disappears. In the same sense the structures out of which the biological entities are made are transient, unstable entities with constantly changing molecules dependent on a constant flow of energy to maintain form and structure.

One can extend this analogy to say that the loss of genetic diversity is a phenomenon decreasing the flow that makes the vortex possible. If the flow becomes too diminished, no more vortex. Why everyone does not feel the pain of Earth's wounding nor the burden of human responsibility for it I cannot say. Perhaps they keep themselves busy so they don't have to hear the great keening. The very fact that most human beings do hear it and grieve and reconsider their love for the world is hopeful. In the way that a brush with death wakes a person up to the deeper values of living, our new insights into the possibility of a miserable and shameful species death may wake us to deeper collective values. Culture now outpaces genes in human evolution. That means we have many choices, a vast capacity for learning, for stopping our planetary killing spree, for redirecting our acquisitive force from things and entertainment toward knowledge and meaning, and for a more gentle relationship with the natural matrix within which we spin.

Spiritual meanings and ethical obligations are emerging with the story that science is giving us: (1) that our existence is possible only within the matrix other lives; (2) that other species have a right to their existence and give meaning to ours; (3) that all life on Earth shares an evolutionary legacy so complex and absolute as to be godly; (4) that nature is sacred and real and central, not peripheral, to human culture; (5) that it is spiritually unacceptable for the creature who invented "beauty," "justice" and "love" not to learn what is necessary in order to live respectfully with other species. If we do not learn this, the human story will end miserably—we will drive ourselves to extinction, taking down much of Earth's beauty and complexity with us. There will be insects and fungi and bacteria left, of course, and who knows what else, to pick around in the garbage. Then in another ten or twenty million years or so, Earth will be strong enough to try again.

One day I visited the California Palace of the Legion of Honor, eating breakfast at the cheesy Golf Club on its grounds—the basic American greasy meat and eggs served on Chinette—while behind my back on a big screen a woman skated to a Muzak

"Claire de Lune." I climbed the hill to join the throng milling in the Rodin gallery, took my turn standing beside *The Mighty Hand* to witness its disembodied force. Then I moved on to *Three Shades*, men (once men) broad with muscular strength, their heads bowed in submission to that beautiful power; then Dave Smith's fist-sized *Head*, welded iron with red paint, just chips and fragments swept from the floor and assembled. Behind me a mother gently explained, "This is how a person would look if you just saw the shapes." *Dancer with Gazelles* had breasts bare and small, the nipples soft, as if they had not yet learned to go erect for sex or feeding, useless and lovely things so nonthreatening they could be guarded by flighty, slender-boned gazelles. And beside her stood *Herakles Drawing His Bow*, legs poised for springing, ferocious, his bare sex like a medicine pouch he proudly carried everywhere.

I left the crowd to wander in the park, found an empty bench facing Golden Gate Bridge, the ruddy steel mechanism no less graceful than gazelles, but stronger than anything born. Beneath the trees, mats of shamrock and spears of new lily green had sprouted with the January rains. Pinecones lined their branches like too many gonads, the long clustered needles waving in the breeze. From the trunk of a giant eucalyptus protruded a magnificent burl, a deformation of the tree that looked like sculpture. And then I saw things the other way around—all the human eagerness and talent to create forms as so much leaf making, lily spear and burl making, bridges and statues and Muzak as our passion to participate in creation no matter the cost. I saw too that form in nature is often a result of damage: the tree's flesh damaged into knots and burls, the ocean's surface damaged into waves, the seed damaged into growth, everything alive damaged into the gift of death. And I saw that I was just part of a story that nature was writing, and if I was lucky I could pick up my pen and scratch a few letters—the poet damaged into form (as Auden wrote of Yeats, "Mad Ireland hurt you into poetry")—and that would be nature's blessed generosity to me before I returned to the wilder place from where I started.

chapter 9

Central City

When human beings gamble
the spirits like to watch.
From the spirit world they laugh
at the winners because winning is a sickness.
They say only losers feel grief.
Only the loser can go home with nothing
& this is a very holy
thing to do.

—Jim Cohn, from *Grasslands*

The tour bus glides along the Peak to Peak Scenic Byway toward Rocky Mountain National Park. It is late April and the trees are spindly gray wood. Red tulips bloom in rectangles and triangles of tended ground. Out beyond the college town, gray mountainsides wear swatches of green-black pine. Monitors hang from the luggage racks of the bus, playing a video while we wind out through suburbs and towns. "You can still find the gold . . ." the voiceover woos, while the camera tracks a yellow aspen leaf floating downstream. "The highest paved road in America . . ." he sings as the camera zooms toward the peaks. And to quell any doubt that traveling on a road might be déclassé in the jet age, the shot goes wide, panning the craggy ridge, then the prairie sloping out below like it will never end, while the voice soars in delight: "Taking a flight by car!" A close-up of miners shows three men chilling out on a ledge eating sandwiches, the narrator finding even in their jobs a touristic delight: "Check out the view they have from their lunchroom!" The formidable rocky spine of the West, the turbulent brown churn and white froth of down-tumbling snowmelt, the silver needle flume of water cascading from the heights, are all here for one purpose—to give joy to the motoring tourist.

But joy is not really what the video is trying to sell. It is trying to sell small towns. The Scenic Byway program was started in 1989 when Colorado was in recession and rural areas were hard hit. Capitalizing on the research finding that driving around in a beautiful landscape is a favorite "outdoor activity" for Americans, planners designated nineteen road trips of scenic and historic significance. The idea was that there were plenty of tourists in the West, but they did not get out to places that most needed an influx of money. The Peak to Peak is the oldest of these designated routes. It runs fifty-five miles and passes through five mountain communities, most of them sparsely settled. The plan did not consider conservation and preservation issues; its goal was economic development. The promotional materials, like the video playing on our tour bus, are filled with whimsy, boosterism and manipulation, aimed to stir the viewer's appetite, not her generosity. No one states the simple fact: these towns are hurting, and if you come here and spend a little money, it will help local residents.

I have come here to attend a conference on tourism sponsored by the Center of the American West at the University of Colorado and to witness the changing face of tourism in the West in the 1990s. Among my fellow passengers are professors of tourism science, recreation and park management, and rural and urban planning, as well as chamber of commerce business boosters, naturalists, historians and citizens concerned about the future of places they love. We are riding the Peak to Peak, stopping in communities along the route to learn what impact the byway program has had on their economy and culture.

There seem to be two extremes of thinking about tourism these days. The dystopian view sees tourism as a capitalistic version of colonialism through which money-wielding invaders demand that locals serve outsiders' whims and desires. The utopian view sees tourism as the means to develop local economies and integrate them into world markets, transforming them from destructive natural-resource-extraction industries to relatively benign service industries. The postmodern thinkers are trying to bring these two views into harmony by advocating local planning based on values: What kinds of exchanges do we wish to foster in our place between hosts and guests? What makes our place unique and valuable to us? What of these qualities are we unwilling to lose for the sake of money? The fact of the matter is that most people love being tourists, and no amount of cranky theorizing about its ill effects will put a damper on this behavior. It is what we do, given a little free time and money. *How* we do it might be improved by considering more respectfully the perspectives of people for whom the place we visit is home.

I have always loved being a tourist, though my preferred style of travel leans toward the maverick meander rather than the guided tour. My first visit to the American West was a road trip I made with my daughter, then thirteen years old, from our home in Vermont to Yellowstone National Park. I drove a rattle-trap pickup truck with a homemade camper on the back, and we budgeted on peanut butter and jelly the whole way, while pouring motor oil into a leaking engine at a frightening rate of consumption. When we got to Yellowstone, the park was closed, all campsites full, so we drove an hour back to a rural Wyoming motel that offered trail rides. I must have feared that at that point in the journey my stock with my daughter might be running low, and since she was in the peak of her horse fetish years, I knew that an hour or two riding horseback would recompense her for all discomfort and disappointment.

We checked in just as the last trail ride of the day was mounting up, two teenage wranglers matching horses and riders in a dusty corral until everyone was in a saddle except me. There were no riderless horses left in sight. The guys looked harried—"Oh, you're coming too?"—eyed each other, then shrugged as if to say "What the hell," and agreed I could ride the muscular buckskin fenced off in a side corral. It was the kind of moment when you know that something important has been left unsaid. Seeing my daughter's joy as the string of ponies began to head for open country, I was grateful, mounted up, and didn't ask any questions, my maternal instinct telling me that this ride was the right thing to do. Between the two of us, my daughter is the only real horsewoman, and this was true even at that stage of her development. What I knew about horses I had learned in order to support her passion for the animal. Back home she had a Shetland pony named Nosy and a quarterhorse-Morgan crossbreed named Traveler. Her discipline and strength with them had earned her a handsome string of 4-H ribbons. And I had been educated by watching her learn to communicate with her hands, her weight and her heels an authority that these powerful animals respected.

We rode out at dusk and returned after sunset, climbing a high desert track through cactus and sage to the edge of a rocky canyon. Down below, one of the wranglers said, they often saw wild mustangs in the evening, sometimes as many as a hundred.

This night there was nothing but the stillness of an empty place where we sat horseback for a while watching the shadows fade into the seeping dark. There were the near sounds of creaking leather, metal chink as a hoof struck stone, wickering of soft lips, bit knocking against teeth, tail whooshing off flies. I was only partly present to this quiet. From the moment I climbed onto that horse, I felt an electricity in his body that I did not entirely trust. I felt it run from his mouth to my hands, felt it against my thighs. I knew that my authority was not a given for this animal, that something wild still ran in his veins, that impulses ran through his body I would be lucky to control. I kept my hands alert to that energy, trying to communicate both respect and strength. The ride was far from a relaxing excursion in the wild. The lead wrangler, probably just a year or two out of high school, had a face and hands already scarred from work. He stuck close to me for most of the ride, and near the end, after we had let the horses lope halfway home and had slowed to cool them, he sidled up beside me, cocked his head and asked, "So how do you like that horse?"

"This is a powerful horse," I replied, throwing him as knowing a look as I could muster.

"Yeah," he said. "That horse killed another horse yesterday."

At such a moment the social code of the West suggests coolness, fearless confidence and camaraderie.

"I knew something was up with him," I said. "What happened?"

But the details of the horse fight were thin and pale compared to the dimension of his disclosure and my newly authentic experience of Western values.

That was twenty years ago, and now I am on a bus in the Rocky Mountains about to hear what the mayor of Nederland, Colorado, population fifteen hundred, has to say about the value of having the Peak to Peak Scenic Byway pass through his community. The mayor has an oval belly, a white fringe of hair surrounding a shiny pate, and the rosy complexion of a man who spends time outside. He wears a canvas-thick cotton shirt the color of bright blue sky. The bus parks at a curbside beside a modest information center, rusted vintage farm implements arrayed for decoration around a small gravel parking lot. Nearby is a small two-decker strip mall—Ace Hardware, Radio Shack, a few local businesses, a weathered slabwood exterior tying them together into one structure. The mayor, an affable man, stands at the front of the bus and tells us that he lives just outside town on the main road. Every day from early summer to late fall, one car per second passes his house. Four million cars per year pass through his town, but not very many of their passengers stop and spend money. He surveyed business owners and found that the longer people had lived there, the less they wanted more development, even if they got their living from it. Some sites along the byways now want demarketing. We're too pretty, they feel, and we don't want that many people to come here. Some want to take themselves off the map.

We stop in Estes Park, not a park at all, but a gateway community to Rocky Mountain National Park. Wild elk graze in the subdivisions, nibbling on geraniums, and a family of bighorns is frozen in bronze on a traffic island. We spend the morning at the Estes Park Convention Center listening to presentations from local residents and tourism planners.

"You don't want to be here in summer," concedes a local businesswoman, describing what happens when a town of five thousand blizzards into the gridlock of twenty-five thousand people a day hitting the streets. The advertising man whose job it is to bring tourists to Estes Park says the community hosts three million people a year. The national park is their "primary product."

They do not want to bring more people to town, but rather to "upgrade the economic value of the people who come here." He says that the new houses built outside town at phenomenal square footage are not appropriate for the area, compromising the views people come here to see. Someone in the audience points out the contradiction that attracting wealthier tourists is likely to lead to more trophy home development.

"Our economic alternatives are none and none," he laments. "That has a calming influence on those of us who want development stopped."

"Where are the environmentalists in your planning?" asks an elderly woman with an angry edge. The local historian says that "special interest groups" were not at the table. This sends the angry woman into a rage.

"The future depends on preserving Colorado, not changing it!"

But the professionals have heard this rage before, and they let it wash over them. *Change is inevitable,* I imagine them thinking, *and how to manage it is the question,* though in each of them there is the memory of some place they regret having lost to change. They are doing their best to be intelligent and sensible, to make room in their minds for something other than money, while outside nature is selling like tabloid news.

The public information officer from Rocky Mountain National Park reminds us that the boundary of the park is political not ecological, and that Estes Park is part of its ecosystem. The National Park has a fifty-million-dollar backlog in maintenance projects, and the biggest concerns are to reduce the visual impact of development along park boundaries, to preserve grazing for populations that move in and out the park, and not to lose the clear Colorado night sky to streetlamps. He says park visitors don't want to pull into a scenic vista and look out onto a development. This is the last land grab in the Rocky Mountain West. He says that the Park Service lacks the backbone to protect the parks, and that Westerners resist government regulation. Park legislation was a double bind from the start, mandated to make its treasures available to all Americans *and* to protect the resources. How can they do both? He says that once an activity becomes part of the economic base, it's very hard to stop—two years ago there were eight hundred thousand commercial overflight tours of Grand Canyon.

"Don't bring your Eastern values out here!" shouts a business booster wearing a fancy bolo. "If people want economic development, they've got to provide things for people to spend money on—the people who need to spend six hundred and fifty dollars a day!"

A regional planner speaks about the problem of the monster home. Not only have too many visitors come to drive around in places where other people are trying to get away from it all. Too many of them have stayed, building monster homes of ten thousand square feet or more and locating them on trophy sites, inflicting a visual blight on scenic vistas. He speaks about the need to educate people about siting and size and design, so that the visual impact is minimized.

An educator snaps back, "Can you *teach* people to be more sensitive? I am an educator by profession, and I don't believe that it works. You have to control development through regulation."

A consultant working to balance economic development with environmental and cultural protection along the byway "corridor" offers, "When buyers are in the frenzy to find a great site, I'd like to ask them how they'll feel if next year someone puts a monster home on the ridge a mile away from them, and how do they think the person who did so last year feels." It is an optimistic wish, aimed at making multiple perspectives a good thing, rather than a source of confusion or contention, but no one sounds very sanguine about halting the seepage of free-market capitalism into the wild West.

We drive on, nearing the summit where a few spindle-thin, windbare ponderosas stand. Snow squall. Sun squall. Trophy home on ridge a mile away—red metal roof—it wants to be seen, not melt into the landscape. "Those people are notorious for their peacocks," sneers a woolly local journalist giving an impromptu tour from the front of the bus. Nearby a 3,700-square-foot church has been proposed, and a mile farther on an 8,100-square-foot house with adjacent swimming pool house. An elderly couple will live there, and they say the house will not be seen from the road. We pass a campground that has twenty-five campsites, slated to grow to 150. "Everyone wants the authentic camping experience," says the journalist, "and now the pall of their campfires blocks the starry sky."

It is not every guided tour that gives one an interpretive lecture on portapotties. But such is the wisdom of this tour's organizers that we make a stop at a rest area outside the rustic village of Allenspark to learn about a recent flare-up in local Peak to Peak politics. Tourists driving the Scenic Byway often had stopped in this village to use rest rooms, but they rarely bought anything. The village had no urban sewer, only local septic systems, so no one was happy about its being the pit stop for all those motorists. The village lobbied the county to build a public rest area outside of town. Once it was built, two neighbors of the facility complained so vehemently about its location that it was moved an eighth of a mile down the road. By the time it was finally functioning to everyone's satisfaction, the plastic outhouse had cost $100,000. It costs $570 a month for maintenance, not including trash removal. On summer days the bright

turquoise cubicle with a snow-white roof is used every four minutes. It needs to be cleaned twice a week. The county pays,
though no one wants to. The moral of the story, the county representative quips ruefully, is "If you build it, they will go."

Our last stop is Central City, one of three former mining
towns now the nexus of corporate casino gambling in Colorado.
Central City, located an hour west of Denver, is not a city and
never has been, but like many gold rush towns it had pretensions
of grandeur. Gilpin County is the smallest, most rural county in
the state, its landscape among the most magnificent in the West:
rugged gray crags rising above dense green forest that spills
down the slopes dwindling into vast grassy plains. One early
travel writer called the area the "Switzerland of America." In
1859, gold was discovered washing down its mountain streams.
Central City, with its sister city Black Hawk one mile away,
boomed. By the turn of the century nearly seven thousand people lived in what was called "the richest square mile on earth."
Gilpin County produced over 4.2 million ounces of gold—at
today's prices a total value of $1.6 billion. The settlers were
mostly Cornish and Welsh miners, their houses climbing up the
towns' steeply terraced hillsides, with gold camps scattered across
the outlying area. The boom was over a few decades later, and the
population began a slow but steady decline until by 1990 fewer
than six hundred people lived in Central City and Black Hawk.

The pioneer settlers of Central City wanted the place to be
more than a crude frontier town. They wanted it to be a good
place to live, a place of culture and refinement. In 1878 they built
an opera house seating 750 people for music festivals and the-
atrical performances. Even well after the gold boom had busted,
the pioneer heirs—at least some of them—cultivated this vision
of their community. In 1932, an effort spirited by long-term residents Ida Kruse McFarland and Anne Evans, working in col-

laboration with Denver society circles, transformed the crumbling old granite theater into the refurbished Central City Opera House. The summer season opened with Lillian Gish starring in *Camille*. On opening night a formal ball was held at the Teller House hotel, bell-ringers walked the streets announcing the performance, and flower girls from Denver's upper crust handed out nosegays to the audience. A new tourist-based economy revolving around a summer festival of the arts and culture had begun. Celebrities came to perform or enjoy the festivities. The town got a new nickname as "the summer theater capital of the U.S." and headlining performers such as Helen Hayes, Sir Michael Redgrave and Beverly Sills upped the cultural ante. Mae West played Diamond Lil in 1949. Visitors lounged around the bars as if they were living rooms. Central City had become a high-class party town.

The Opera House Association worked with Denver officials and money to extend its efforts to historic preservation, buying and restoring many older Victorian homes and relics of mining culture. Some promoted the vision of Central City as "the American Salzburg" and hoped to turn the whole town into a preserved site like Williamsburg, Virginia, celebrating the mining history of the Old West. Not all the locals agreed with this vision of the future or of their past. The old miners in town in particular were not impressed with having city folks use their town as a playground. The implication of the "historic" perspective was that the place was dead, except during the few summer months when the socialites arrived, an image many locals found false and degrading. Dissenting locals objected to tax breaks given to the Opera House Association and argued that these outsiders had little interest in the community's needs. The conflict bubbled up into a feud. In 1948, Central City residents tried to recall their mayor for giving special concessions to the association.

The recall failed, but the fight continued. In fact, tourism scholar Patricia Stokowski reports that in conducting research for her book, *Riches and Regrets: Betting on Gambling in Two Colorado Mining Towns,* she found that even in the early 1990s the hostility had not abated. Locals called the Opera House Association folks "snooty," claiming that "they lord it over us," and association members described locals as "provincial" and "unfriendly." But the summer festival season was not a sufficient economic base to offer much stability to Central City. While the town enjoyed some benefit from the growth of tourism through the 1950s and 1960s, by the 1980s it had become remote and tired, its historical buildings falling down and most of it mining structures gone.

Small-town life has cachet for Americans, at least in their fantasies. It represents the romance of living in a community of like-minded others. The imaginary place is steeped in natural beauty and tranquillity, and those who live there do so because they want to, not because they have to. There are common stories about the past—about the heroes and heroines who made the place what it is and how they got there, about the frenzied lives of city folks who don't know the value of the commonplace, about local eccentrics who are tolerated or pitied but not feared. No one locks doors. The stories are exchanged at the post office, or at the corner store, or in passing on the street. Everyone knows the neighbors. Hatreds and jealousies are dismissed with an anecdote and a harmless sneer, because people want to respect one another's differences. I won't challenge your individual rights if you won't challenge mine, because we all have come here to celebrate how independent we are, how much we respect an intimate scale of human enterprise, unlike those corporate lemmings in the city.

Beyond the romance there are drawbacks to small-town life—

scarce job opportunities, low wages, few cultural resources, limited services and amenities, barely repressed historical hostilities, and a cloyingly narrow sense of expectations. It is worst for the youth, because no matter how much they love the place and have become decent people because of it, they know that if they want to make something of themselves, they have to leave. Add to that the physical hardships of the climate in the Rocky Mountain West and the difficulty of commuting daily through winter snow and ice to the city, and it is not surprising that the romance of small-town life has not been sufficient to keep places like Central City thriving. The monster homes being built in outlying areas are usually second or third homes, or retirement homes, and their owners are not strongly invested in the civic affairs of nearby small towns. They can enjoy the pleasures of rural life on their own terms, without undue hardship or social obligation. If they are electronically plugged in, they need feel no sense of cultural isolation. Their personal and professional relationships can be fostered at the keyboard, and their sense of community will increasingly become not one of place, but one of placeless electronic affiliation. They are the very models of American independence and individualism and free choice.

According to Stokowski, the first public mention of gambling in Central City appeared in the local paper in September 1989 when its mayor, Bruce Schmalz, was quoted as saying, "If kept small . . . legalized gambling . . . could provide jobs, being a real boost to a slumping economy." What was proposed was a mom-and-pop-scale operation, "a few slot machines in every business," with proceeds to be earmarked for historic preservation. Gambling had been a part of many frontier towns in Colorado. During the first legislative session of the territorial government in 1861, and in several subsequent years, a number of bills had been passed that increasingly restricted gambling. But the laws were enforced or ignored as the ethical climate varied. Prohibitions relaxed gradually, as elsewhere in the nation. In 1949 horse and dog track betting were legalized in the state, in 1983 a state lottery was approved, and in 1990 a statewide referendum was approved allowing limited-stakes gambling (slot machines, poker and blackjack, with no bets exceeding five dollars) in the towns of Central City, Black Hawk and Cripple Creek. Shortly after the bill passed, buttons went on sale in town reading "The Boom Is Back in Gilpin County!" As Western historian Patricia Nelson Limerick has written, "mining set a mood that has never disappeared from the West: the attitude of extractive industry—get in, get rich, get out."

Our tour bus gears down descending into Gregory Gulch, the side street edging the ravine in which Central City is sandwiched. We creep along in a string of casino shuttle vans and tour buses from Denver, stopping just short of a covered portico in front of a block-long four-story building that looks almost historic, maybe an old office building or apartment house. In fact, from the streets, everything in Central City looks almost historic. Victorian clapboard or brick facades in rowhouse array, varied roof heights, small sash windows, all looking a bit new and oversized for a mining town. On this street there is only one building that is actually historic, a small, dark, steeply roofed one-story structure poking out of a phalanx of giants. In scale it looks like a lone egret standing knee-high in a cattle stampede. We unload at Harvey's, our tour leader handing each of us a casino coupon for five dollars' worth of free quarters and marching orders that we'll have time to play the machines or wander the streets after the planned presentations in the conference room. We thread through the confusion of loading and unloading vehicles and enter the casino just as a wizened couple is leaving—the woman arthritic and hardly able to walk, her husband carrying an oxygen canister, canula clipped to his nose. "Ka-ching, ka-ching," she says to me playfully, shaking her cardboard coin bucket, her face lit with impish joy. Add a bit of glamour, take away the oxygen, and this is the image that the industry promotes—gambling is good, clean fun and entertainment.

Inside the Victorian skin of the casino sprawls a cavernous expanse of blinking, spinning, clicking, flashing gizmos, an electronic organism bent on making those who enter lose their money and have a good time doing it. The place is intentionally disorienting, and we are like the little steel balls rolling inside a pinball machine, bouncing past one clanking device after another, as if we have nowhere to go, but are rolling downhill toward a narrow black chute where the motion and noise will stop, until someone puts another quarter in the slot. These small-town casinos provide a feeder market for the big-time industry showplaces in Vegas and Reno. But small or grand, one principle applied to all casino design is to close out external stimuli: little or no daylight, no clocks, and breakfast served all day long. Breakfast is an important detail, because to eat breakfast is to prepare for the new day, to leave yesterday's losses behind, and begin with the optimism of morning. In casinoland, it is morning all day long.

I once visited the Silver Legacy in Reno, at the urging of friend and colleague, Scott Slavic, who runs the dynamic new graduate program in literature and the environment at the University of Nevada in Reno. We rode the escalator up past a theatrically whimsical reproduction of a silver mine, carloads of faux ore running from the blinking top of a mountain down a spiraling track to dump out below as coins in a bank of slot machines. We stood at the railing of an open amphitheater to gaze overhead at the domed sky where twenty-four virtual hours would pass in every two hours of real time—rosy sunrise, bright midday, storm clouds building and exploding in afternoon, peaceful sunset, then magnificent night—a time-lapse experience that promised promptly to refresh every gambler's fantasy of the bets going better tomorrow. So far in Central City, however, there is no grand technological theater in the casinos, only room after room, floor after floor, of ka-ching, ka-ching, ka-ching. The next wave of development promises Roman and tropical themes, complete with indoor waterfalls and palm trees.

We retreat to the quiet of an upstairs conference room to consider three perspectives on the role of gambling development in rural community sustainability. Patricia Stokowski studies and teaches at Texas A&M about social and cultural impacts of tourism. She is professional and tight-lipped, plain-looking, though she wears a hot pink blazer, black crepe slacks, and a pink floral silk scarf. She is cold in her knowledge, though not passionless. Perhaps she has learned to affect coldness in order to withstand the heat of public debate. She knows the facts and the story of this place better than anyone else in the room. Stokowski's research on Central City began before the casinos came to town and continued through opening day. She says that the casino industry swept into these towns because the locals could never agree on what kind of development they wanted. Composed of independent-minded Westerners, the citizenry hated regional planning exercises that always seemed to serve the business interests of local politicians, and they hated being told by outsider experts what to do. Their commitment to local history, as she wrote in *Riches and Regrets,*

> *tended to be expressed primarily in terms of personal freedoms rather than by collective participation in community projects or civic improvements. People lived in Gilpin County because it offered a peaceful mountain environ-*

ment away from the city, escape from the social conven-
tions and laws of other places, and few constraints on in-
dividualism.

She analyzes the strategies used by gambling proponents. "Diversionary reframing" countered opponents' concerns not with discussion of the merits and problems of gambling development but with angry rebuttals and name-calling. "They just want our community to remain impoverished!" Opponents were cast as anti-growth, anti-progress, un-American. "The rhetoric of despair" depicted Central City as a dying, desperate town with no other options, though data do not confirm that this was the case. A Citizen Study conducted in 1990 concluded that though the towns had been in decline for half a century, they had grown substantially in the past thirty years. Many residents worked outside the county at professional jobs, were highly educated and had substantial incomes. They owned large homes in county subdivisions outside town. Those people not doing so well were the elderly and the marginally employed—generally people living in town, and the ones who would be displaced by casino development. "Historical commoditization" promised to bring back the "Old Wild West" spirit (though Central City had been a workplace and cultural center, never a "Wild West" town), to turn gambling profits into historic preservation funds, and to attract tourists not just for gambling but also to learn about the historic and cultural heritage of the place. When "growth machine politics" began to roll in like a tumbleweed, it could not be stopped. What was created, Stokowski says, was "a historyless place pretending to be historical," as original buildings were destroyed, or mysteriously collapsed during restoration, in order to make way for big operators. Property owners rode the swell of increased real estate values, but other locals—the elderly, renters, trailer park residents—had no voice as free-market capitalism flooded the town. Since gambling began no one has celebrated the day gold was discovered in Central City. Rather, local government leaders announced in 1994 that a troupe of provocative "Shady Ladies of the Motherlode" would be the "city ambassadors" to celebrate the "role of successful business women of the Old West." The real history of pioneer women and Victorian society ladies was not considered as "authentic" (for development purposes) as a fabricated history of ubiquitous "ladies of the night."

We hear from the planning director of neighboring Black Hawk, a casual young man in chinos and open-collared striped shirt. Hardly a futurist, he looks beaten by what he has experienced, as if knowing that as a planner for a town now utterly dependent on corporate gambling he is a classic case of the tail wagging the dog.

"Seven years ago," he says, "there were one hundred and eighty people living in Black Hawk. Everyone knew everyone by their first name, and half were related by blood or marriage. Now there are ten thousand strangers in the streets and your next-door neighbor is a multimillionaire. We had five hundred and fifty thousand square feet of development in four years, and eighty percent of it is business funded by Nevada corporations."

But, he urges, we should compare the environmental impact of mining, which slashed and polluted the land. We should look at the good use of mass transit in town. We should remember the hardships of mining life, the diseases and accidents. There are things you put up with in every way of life.

"What are your planning priorities for the next five to ten years?" I ask, looking for a thread of hope.

"Infrastructure and diversification of business," he replies. "And developing service communities in outlying towns, because now those properties in Black Hawk are economically out-classed. There isn't even a gas station in town."

He did not sound hopeful, beyond his professional obligation to do so. The town is again invested in one industry and newly vulnerable to the cycle of boom and bust. Locals can no longer start a business, because property owners will only rent month to month, in hopes that a casino might come in and rent or buy from them at top dollar. The state, which is responsible for regulating gambling, is now dependent on gambling tax revenues, with which it finances public works. Ironically, public coffers have much to gain by what private citizens lose in casinos. The much-touted funding of historic preservation has benefited other communities in Colorado, but the three rural towns given over to gambling have been sacrificed. The fate of Central City, Black Hawk and Cripple Creek now depends upon nonlocal corporate interests whose bottom lines are a sum of their enterprises in Las Vegas, Reno, New Orleans and wherever else they have established "gaming" (the industry-wide word that washes away any last taints of moral judgment attached to "gambling") operations. Local planning in these towns is no longer a matter of neighbors trying to sit down together and iron out their differences. The opportunity for that scale of planning came and went unrealized.

There were alternatives for Central City and her sister towns. Stokowski points out that there were models of more limited ventures available,

> *from the British model of pub gambling, to the Deadwood [South Dakota] model of thirty devices per building, to the continental model of one large casino per city or resort. Certainly the more stringent development of one large casino in Central City and another in Black Hawk, with*

*revenues going to local town and county governments and
local historic restoration, would have reduced all forms of
negative impacts. Mechanisms for limiting growth are
available, but whether the community has the political
will to enact these remains an issue.*

Among the tourist interests other than gambling that rank high
in recent surveys are cultural and learning experiences, experiences of "authenticity" and "integrity." And Central City might
have capitalized on this national and international market had it
agreed upon a plan for development that would enhance not
only its economics, but also its culture. Now the place is a cau-
tionary tale: if locals cannot agree on what things they are collectively unwilling to sacrifice for the sake of money, corporate
interests are ready, willing and able to step into the breech, and
such interests, in all but the rarest cases, will sacrifice anything
and everything for money.

Finally we hear from the representative of Harvey's in Central
City. He is slick and cocksure, a spinmaster in pressed rayon and
silk. He is working his way up and glows with how well he is
doing. He tells us that 15 percent of the U.S. population cite
"gaming" as their favorite leisure-time activity, making it sound
like a harmless hobby. Gambling, however, is nothing like a
hobby, because it is fostered not by individual avocation but by
an aggressive industry rapidly developing and promoting new
markets. During 1994 in Colorado $3.9 million was spent on
gambling; in Nevada $96.9 million.

"We haven't hit everyone in the market," he says, optimistic
about future growth, though grousing about how heavily the industry is taxed. Harvey's pays 20 percent of every dollar it makes
to the state. Still, the numbers are on his side: 15 percent of the
population of Denver would rather play slot machines than go

to the movies; that's three hundred thousand people. That's the target group, though the company factors in, when considering potential profits, the number of daily flights leaving Denver for Vegas.

"We know all the demographics about our players," he says when someone in the audience challenges his calculations. Someone else asks about compulsive gamblers, and he says he has just been elected to the board of a group to help them.

"But," he laughs, "some people exercise every day—it's what they like to do."

"This would be a terrifying place to raise a child!" shouts a woman in the audience.

"Heh, heh," he mimics, "like Rodney Dangerfield says, this is tough crowd. But, really, parents like the new quality of life here. Gaming is entertaining! This is just like any other resort. And now there are more police on the streets—"

"That's because crime has risen," Stokowski asserts, citing rapid increases in property crimes, aggravated assaults and drug arrests. "Gambling tourists are not ski resort tourists."

"How can you call this a resort?" shouts the accusatory woman. "No one under age twenty-one can enter!"

"Hey," says Mr. Casino, raising his palms and smiling in mock self-defense, "this is a work in progress. We're only six years old. We have plans for a video arcade and a child care center. This is what the consumer wants!"

Not *this* consumer, I think, and knowing that I cannot contain my rage any longer and that I do not want to self-immolate in public, I storm out. I pace the streets looking for anything not swept into this new simulacrum of a town. On a hillside away from the hubbub I find the Thomas Historical House Tour with its dumbed-down slogan, "Walk Thru a House Froze in Time." But the house is closed. In the storefront window of an old drugstore dwarfed between ka-chinging neighbors hang a few milky historic photographs. One shows a funeral procession leading up to St. Mary's Church. Fourteen men had been killed by shaft-rupture flood in the Americus and Sleepy Hollow mines on August 29, 1895. And here is the line of stagecoaches, the women wearing long, full-skirted black dresses, the children clustered around. There is a picture taken maybe thirty years later of men working on a railroad track. The town had become so poor that they pulled up its tracks to sell for scrap. And now the storefront where the photos hang is for sale.

chapter 10

Poetry and Science: A View from the Divide

The most remarkable discovery made by scientists is science itself. The discovery must be compared in importance with the invention of cave-painting and writing. Like these earlier human creations, science is an attempt to control our surroundings by entering into them and understanding them from inside. And like them, science has surely made a critical step in human development and cannot be reversed.

—Jacob Bronowski

In this book I have tracked my experiences of nature and culture as I have encountered them during a period of travel and questioning. Historically, cultures have been formed by places, by the natural features and resources available to people living in a specific geographic habitat. "The globalization of culture" is the term in fashion for the phenomenon of everyone becoming more contiguous, contingent, and more like us. We lament the dilution of local cultures in the floodwaters of global capitalism, feel a justifiable panic about the pace of this change, and wonder how we will know ourselves and others in the future if our nationalistic and ethnic identities melt away. It is not a contradiction that people by the droves are looking for their own cultural roots, castigating others for past cultural injustices, and documenting difference wherever they can find it, at a time when place-based culture is fading fast. We know something archetypal and precious is leaking out of the world.

But culture is not only place-based. Culture is also based on discipline, profession, affinity and taste, and in these forms has been around since the beginning of civilization. The problem with the future is that it is difficult to know what will happen there. But it seems likely that these non-place-based forms of culture will become increasingly important. Culture will become more and more our habitat, as cultural learning continues to supplant the poky genetic code. I am not suggesting that we relax our vigilance in protecting actual places and preserving the knowledge acquired by deeply place-based cultures, only that our motivation and ability to do these things may change—may even improve—as new cross-cultural affinities emerge. My affinities for literary writers and natural scientists probably say at least as much about who I am as the geographic fact that I am a tenth-generation New Englander, and nourish me in ways that make my best work possible. Cultural exchanges across disciplinary boundaries can be as fruitful as those across geographic ones. Unlike C. P. Snow, I do not see "the intellectual life of the whole of western society being split into two polar groups," literary intellectuals at one pole and scientists at another. I have always been struck, perhaps naively, by the fundamental similarity between the poet and the scientist: both are seeking a language for the unknown.

The great English poet John Donne published "An Anatomy of the World" in 1611, one year after Galileo's first accounts of his work with the telescope appeared. The poem was probably commissioned as a funeral elegy for Elizabeth Drury, who died at age fourteen, the daughter of a wealthy London landowner. But that loss is not the only spiritual dislocation the poem commemorates. The universe suddenly had been peppered with ten times the stars that had been there before. The perception of the earth's place in that expanded (though not yet expanding) universe had been thrown into metaphysical revolution. Donne was not convinced by the new theories of Copernicus and Brahe placing the sun at the center and the earth as merely a whirling outlier, but he took them seriously enough that one can feel his inner sense reeling. An excerpt of the poem goes like this:

> And new philosophy calls all in doubt,
> The element of fire is quite put out;
> The sun is lost, and th' earth, and no man's wit
> Can well direct him where to look for it.
> And freely men confess that this world's spent,
> When in the planets, and the firmament
> They seek so many new . . .
> 'Tis all in pieces, all coherence gone. . . .

Part of his task as a poet was to integrate this new information about the nature of reality with his beliefs and emotions, to give a voice to his very process of confusion, his struggle for equilibrium in a newly unstable world. It is difficult to imagine a conceptual change more profound than the one experienced during the first century of modern science. The Copernican Revolution meant that people could no longer trust their senses. The experience of observing the sun circle around the earth, as one might continue to witness every day, was no longer the truth. What then could be the value of the senses, of experience, after one has learned that the truth requires tests, measurement and collective scrutiny?

That shift in earthlings' fundamental sense of place may not seem like a big deal now. We have had a few centuries to get used to living with its psychic disjunction. But science (along with its headstrong, profiteering offspring technology) has not slowed down in presenting artists with destabilizing new realities. As we race toward the millennium, the dizzying changes in chaos and quantum and genome theories, in the neurophysics of the brain and the biotechnology of reproduction, and in the search for the Theory of Everything can send the amateur science-watcher into a state of permanent vertigo. Indeed, I am surprised at how few contemporary artists, and in particular poets, have captured that sense of reeling. Certainly there are some—A. R. Ammons, Richard Kenney, Pattiann Rogers, James Merrill, Diane Ackerman, Miroslav Holub, May Swenson, Jorie Graham and Loren Eiseley all have made footholds in the shifting terrain.

Nevertheless, the view from either side of the disciplinary divide seems to be that poetry and science are fundamentally opposed, if not hostile to one another. Scientists are seekers of fact; poets revelers in sensation. Scientists seek a clear, verifiable and elegant theory; contemporary poets, as critic Helen Vendler recently put it, create objects that are less and less like well-wrought urns, and more and more like the misty collisions and diffusions that take place in a cloud chamber. The popular view demonizes us both, perhaps because we serve neither the god of profit-making nor the god of usefulness. Scientists are the cold-hearted dissectors of all that is beautiful; poets the lunatic heirs to pagan forces. We are made to embody the mythic split in Western civilization between the head and the heart. But none of this divided thinking rings true to my experience as a poet.

In my high school biology notebook, which I keep among the few artifacts of my youth that continue to interest me, among the drawings in meticulous colored pencil of the life cycles of diploblastic coelenterates and hermaphroditic annelids, is a simple schematic of an unspecified point in human history at which science and religion took separate paths as ways to understand the world. I still can picture my biology teacher with his waxy crewcut and sport jacket standing at the blackboard explaining the schism as simply as if it were an intersection on a highway. What could be tested and measured took the road of science, he said, and the unknown took the other. It is the drawing I remember most keenly because it seemed to me, even then, puzzling. How could the great questions about the nature of existence be separated into subjects, professions, vocabularies that had little to say to one another? Wasn't everyone, wasn't all knowledge and ignorance, joined by the simple desire to know the physical world, to learn how "I" got to be a part of it, and to make some meaning out of our collective existence? How would the world look, I wondered, if one could see it from a point prior to that split?

I was hooked. Science became for me, not the precinct of facts, but the place where the most interesting questions were asked. I knew that no matter how much the professional rigor of science demanded objectivity, there would always be the curiosity and bewilderment of a human being hiding somewhere in the data. And though decades would pass before I heard the name Heisenberg, I already began to sense what I would later read: that "even in science the object of research is no longer nature itself, but man's investigation of nature."

That year for the school science fair I conducted an experiment on white mice to see if they would get skin cancer from tobacco. I distilled the smoke of cigarettes into a vile black paste and spread it on their pink depilatoried backs. For the control, I used a known carcinogen, benzanthracene, I believe. I kept the cages in the cellar playroom of my family's home, tucked on top of the piano. All of my subjects developed lesions. I was a smoker at the time (a fact that did not favorably impress the fair's judges). After the fair, my biology teacher, also a smoker, helped me etherize my charges. And that's about the extent of my career as a scientist—a far cry from the lofty questions that had spurred my interest. The experience led, twenty years later, to the poem "Science," in which I began to discover the mythology of science as a guiding force in our civilization, a force like that of ancient gods, capable of generating both transforming hope and abject humility, a discipline that explores both the nature of reality and the nature of ourselves.

It is the mythological significance of science that continues to attract me as a poet, not simply the guiding stories and metaphors—the Big Bang, the Tangled Bank, and the Neural Jungle—but also the questions that drive scientific endeavor, the ambiguities and uncertainties it produces. No one with a television can fail to perceive that current scientific events play a prominent role in American culture, whether we understand the events or not. The incredible staying power of *Star Trek,* in all its combinations and permutations and spinoff subculture, attests to this. Where will those wacky intergalactic science nerds lead us next? But an actual science event—news of research, for example, with the Hubble Space Telescope, the genome-mapping project, biogenetic engineering or the extinction of species—meets more than its share of the public's hostility and skepticism toward authority of any stripe. Today fewer Americans than ever believe scientists' warnings about global warming and diversity loss. Their skepticism stems, in part, from the fact that to a misleading extent the process of science does not get communicated in the media. What gets communicated is uncertainty, a necessary stage in solving complex problems, not synonymous with ignorance. But the discipline itself is called into question when a scientist tells the truth and says, in response to a journalist's prodding, "Well, we just don't know the answer to that question."

The public's skepticism stems from other sources. Everyone knows all too well that an expert can be found (and paid) to take any scientific position that will support the claim of a special (likely corporate) interest. Coupled with this, the public is generally ignorant about the most basic science concepts. In a 1995 study fewer than 10 percent of U.S. adults could describe a molecule, only 20 percent could minimally define DNA, and slightly fewer than half knew that Earth rotates around the sun once a year. Lacking basic science literacy, one is unable to assess whether or not an expert opinion is persuasive. The capacity to appreciate such tropes as "the selfish gene," "punctuated equilibrium," "the greenhouse effect" or "cascading extinctions" is beyond hope.

What science-bashers fail to appreciate is that scientists, in their unflagging attraction to the unknown, *love* what they don't know. It guides and motivates their work; it keeps them up late at night; and it makes that work poetic. As Nobel Prize–winning poet Czeslaw Milosz has written, "The incessant striving of the mind to embrace the world in the infinite variety of its forms with the help of science or art is, like the pursuit of any object of desire, erotic. Eros moves both physicists and poets." Both the evolutionary biologist and the poet participate in the inherent tendency of nature to give rise to pattern and form.

In addition to the questing of science, its language also attracts me—the beautiful particularity and musicality of the vocabulary, as well as the star-factory energy with which the discipline gives birth to neologisms. I am wooed by words such as "hemolymph," "zeolite," "cryptogam," "sclera," "xenotransplant" and "endolithic," and I long to save them from the tedious syntax in which most science writing imprisons them. As a friend from across the divide has confirmed, even over there the condition of "journal-induced narcolepsy" is all too well known. The flourishing of literary science writers, including Rachel Carson, Lewis Thomas, E. O. Wilson, Oliver Sacks, James Gleick, Stephen Jay Gould, Gary Paul Nabhan, Evelyn Fox Keller, Natalie Angier, David Quammen, Stephen Hawking, Terry Tempest Williams and Robert Michael Pyle, attests to the fruitfulness of harvesting this vocabulary, of finding means other than the professional journal for communicating the experience of doing science. I mean, in particular, those aspects of the experience that will not fit within rigorous professional constraints—for example, the personal story of what calls one to a particular kind of research, the boredom and false starts, the search for meaningful patterns within randomness and complexity, professional friendships and rivalries, the unrivaled joy of making a discovery, the necessity for metaphor and narrative in communicating a theory, and the applications and ethical ramifications of one's findings. Ethnobotanist and writer Gary Paul Nabhan, one of the most gifted of these disciplinary cross-thinkers, asserts that "narrative and metaphor are more honest, precise and comprehensive ways of explaining an animal's life history than the standard technical format of hypothesis, materials, methods, results and discussion."

Much is to be gained when scientists raid the evocative techniques of literature, and when poets raid the language and mythology of scientists. The challenge for a poet is not merely to pepper the lines with spicy words and facts, but to know enough science that the concepts and vocabulary become part of the fabric of one's mind, so that in the process of composition a metaphor or paradigm from the domain of science is as likely to crop up as is one from literature or her own backyard. I subscribe to *Science News* to foster that process, not for total comprehension, but to pick up fibers and twigs, so to speak, that I might tuck into the nest of my imagination.

Here is a recent poem of mine that operates on this principle, a poem that pokes fun at some of the rather curious practices of my naturalist friends, while praising the deeper longing that motivates them.

THE NATURALISTS

When the naturalists
see a pile of scat,
they speed toward it
as if a rare orchid
bloomed in their path.
They pick apart
the desiccated turds,
retrieving a coarse
black javelina hair
or husk of piñon nut
as if unearthing gems.
They get down on their knees
to nose into flowers
a micron wide—belly flowers,
they say, because that's
what you get down on
to see them. Biscuitroot,
buffalo gourd, cryptogams
to them are hints of
some genetic memory
fossilized in their brains,
an ancient music they try

to recall because,
although they can't quite
hear the tune, they know
if they could sing it
that even their own wild
rage and lust and death
terrors would seem
as beautiful as the
endolithic algae
that releases nitrogen
into rocks so that
junipers can milk them.

I will leave the analysis, both literary and psychological, to the critics. What pleases me about this poem (other than the fact that I managed to use both "cryptogam" and "endolithic" in a single poem) is the way that an interesting fact (that rock-dwelling algae are a major source of nutrient for junipers growing in rim-rock country) becomes a metaphor for inner, meditative aspects of the naturalists' work. As Leo Kadanoff wrote, "It is an experience like no other experience I can describe, the best thing that can happen to a scientist, realizing that something that's happened in his or her mind exactly corresponds to something that happens in nature." And so it is with poets.

But science and poetry, when each discipline is practiced with integrity, use language in a fundamentally different manner. Both disciplines share the attempt to find a language for the unknown, to develop an orderly syntax to represent accurately some carefully seen aspect of the world. Both employ language in a manner more distilled than ordinary conversation. Both, at their best, use metaphor and narrative to make unexpected connections. But, as Czech immunologist and poet Miroslav Holub points out, "For the sciences, words are an auxiliary tool." Science—within the tradition of its professional literature—uses language for verification and counts on words to have a meaning so specific that they will not be colored by feelings and biases. Science uses language as if it were another form of measurement—exact, definitive and logical. The unknown, for science, is in nature. Poetry uses language itself as the object—as Valéry said, poems are made with words, not ideas—and counts on the imprecision of words to create accidental meanings and resonances. The unknown, for poetry, is in language. Each poem is an experiment to see if language can convey a shapely sense of the swarm of energy buzzing through the mind. The elegance and integrity of a scientific theory has to do with the exclusion of subjective, emotional factors. The elegance and integrity of a poem is created, to a great extent, by its tone, the literary term used to describe the emotional hue of a poem conveyed by the author's style. The aim of scientific communication is to present results to the reader, preferably results that could be obtained by another researcher following the same procedures; the aim of poetry is to produce a subjective experience, one that could be obtained through no other means than the unique arrangement of elements that make up the poem. Perhaps, among scientific specialties, the work of evolutionary biologists comes closest to that of poets, because its object of study (the biological past) is intangible, its method narrative: to tell the story of life on earth.

While the two disciplines employ language in different ways, they are kindred in their creative process. W.I.B. Beveridge, a British animal pathologist, has written several useful books about the mental procedures that lead to new ideas, whether in science, art or any other imaginative enterprise. "Most discoveries that break new ground," he asserts, "are by their very nature unforeseeable." The process is not purely rational, but dependent upon chance, intuition and imagination. He analyzes the part that chance plays by delineating three different types of discovery in which it is a vital factor: intuition from random juxtaposition of ideas, which is an entirely mental process; eureka intuition, which results from interaction of mental activity with the external world; and serendipity, which is found externally without an active mental contribution.

Random intuition links apparently unconnected ideas or information to form a new, meaningful relationship. It is like those children's books with the pages split in half. You combine a lumberjack's torso with a ballerina's legs, and—presto—a chimera is born. Eureka intuition is best represented by two classic examples. While visiting the baths, Archimedes suddenly awoke to a significant principle that would enable him to measure the volume of an object based upon the amount of water it displaced. At the time he had been wrestling with a royal problem. The ruler Hiero suspected that he had been cheated by the goldsmith who had crafted his crown. Archimedes' job was to determine the volume of the crown, so as to learn, from its weight, whether or not it had been made of pure gold. The Roman architect Vitruvius recounts the eureka moment of Archimedes' discovery:

> *When he went down into the bathing pool he observed that the amount of water which flowed outside the pool was equal to the amount of his body that was immersed. Since this fact indicated the method of explaining the case, he did not linger, but moved with delight he leapt out of the pool, and going home naked, cried aloud that he had found exactly what he was seeking. For as he ran he shouted in Greek: eureka, eureka.*

The second classic example is that of Isaac Newton, who watched an apple fall from a tree and saw in its motion the same force that governs the moon's attraction to the earth. Eureka intuitions occur, Beveridge explains, when one *"seeks* random stimulation from outside the problem," and they "evoke the exclamation 'I have found it!' "

In serendipity one finds something one had not been looking for: an unusual event, a curious coincidence, an unexpected result to an experiment. The term was coined by Horace Walpole in 1754 after an ancient fairy tale that told of the three Princes of Serendip. "They were always making discoveries, by accident and sagacity, of things which they were not in quest of. . . . you must observe that *no* discovery of a thing you *are* looking for ever comes under this description." Examples of serendipity are Columbus finding the New World when he was seeking the Orient, and Fleming discovering penicillin when mold accidentally grew on his discarded staphylococcus culture plates. For discoveries to be made by serendipity, more is required than luck. Beveridge emphasizes that "accidents *and* sagacity" are involved: one must be keenly observant, adventuresome, ready to change one's mind or one's goal.

I think of poetry as a means to study nature, as is science. Not only do many poets find their subject matter and inspiration in the natural world, but the poem's enactment is itself a study of wildness, since art is the materialization of the inner life, the truly wild territory that evolution has given us to explore. Poetry is a means to create order and form in a field unified only by chaos; it is an act of resistance against the second law of thermodynamics that says, essentially, that everything in the universe is running out of steam. And if language is central to human evolution, as many theorists hold, what better medium could be found for studying our own interior jungle? Because the medium of poetry is language, no art (or science) can get closer to embodying the uniqueness of a human consciousness. While neuroscientists studying human consciousness may feel hampered by their methodology because they never can separate the subject and object of their study, the poet works at representing both subject and object in a seamless whole and, therefore, writes a science of the mind.

I find such speculation convincing, which is probably why I became a poet and not a scientist. I could never stop violating the most basic epistemological assumption of science: that we can understand the natural world better if we become objective. Jim Armstrong, writing in a recent issue of *Orion*, puts his disagreement with this assumption and its moral implications more aggressively:

> *Crudely put, a phenomenon that does not register on some instrument is not a scientific phenomenon. So if the modern corporation acts without reference to "soul," it does so guided by scientific principles—maximizing the tangibles (profit, product output) that it can measure, at the expense of the intangibles (beauty, spiritual connectedness, sense of place) that it cannot. . . .*

Clearly a divide separates the disciplines of science and poetry. In many respects we cannot enter one another's territory. The divide is as real as a rift separating tectonic plates or a border separating nations. But a border is both a zone of exclusion and a zone of contact where we can exchange some aspects of our difference, and, like neighboring tribes who exchange seashells and obsidian, obtain something that is lacking in our own locality.

One danger to our collective well-being is that language continues to become more specialized within professional disciplines to the extent that we become less and less able to understand one another across the many divides, and the general public becomes less and less willing to try to understand what any of the experts are saying.

Writing the Lowell lectures at Harvard in 1925, Alfred North Whitehead foresaw the dangers of specialization. In his work on the metaphysical foundations of science, *Science and the Modern World*, the mathematician cautioned that with increasing scientific and technological refinements "the specialized functions of the community are performed better and more progressively, but the generalized direction lacks vision. The progressivism in detail only adds to the danger produced by the feebleness of coordination . . . in whatever sense you construe the meaning of community . . . a nation, a city, a district, an institution, a family or even an individual. . . . The whole is lost in one of its aspects."

The whole that we are losing is the belief in the integrity of life. We may have confidence in the earth's fecundity, its cleverness in reinventing life even after cataclysmic extinction spasms. But we are coming to suspect that the future of humanity is a detail that is at odds with the well-being of the whole. "If present trends continue," Beveridge wrote in 1980, "only about 1 percent of the Earth's surface will remain in its natural state by the turn of the century and a large proportion of the animal species will be doomed to extinction." Civilization is speeding up the process of evolution so fiercely that species counting on their genes to keep up lose ground as fast as we either claim or ruin it.

In addition to widespread species loss, the planet is experiencing widespread loss of cultures and languages. Jared Diamond, in a 1993 article, wrote that at the present rate of loss the world's six thousand modern languages could be reduced within a century or two to just a few hundred. He estimates that it takes over a million speakers for a language to be secure. The majority of languages are "little" ones having around five thousand speakers, and they are fostered by geographic isolation. The Americas at the time of the Conquest had one thousand languages; Diamond speculates that there may have been tens of thousands of languages spoken before the expansion of farmers began around eight thousand years ago. As remote regions become less remote, the little languages erode. Since each language represents not merely a vocabulary and set of syntactical rules but a unique way of seeing the world, these losses diminish our collective heritage.

Yet one can take some heart that specialized vocabularies within the large languages are burgeoning, and in no field are they doing so with more gusto than in science, providing fresh instruments for seeing the world. And as Whitehead wrote, "A fresh instrument serves the same purpose as foreign travel; it shows things in unusual combinations. The gain is more than a mere addition; it is a transformation."

For both science and poetry the challenges lie in taking on the complexity of the most interesting questions (formal, technical, theoretical and moral) within our fields without losing connection with people outside of our fields. The idea of poetry with which I grew up was, I suppose, a particularly American one— that is, as an escape from the burdens of community into extreme individuality, a last bastion of rugged individualism from which one could fire salvos at an ever more remote, corrupt and inane culture. Historically, however, the voice of poetry has not always been construed to be the heightened voice of individualism. Among the original forms of humanity, art was unified with prayer and healing science. Poems and songs were manifestations of a collective voice, of spells and visions, of spirits returning from the dead. Such poetry transcended individualism, rather than celebrating it. We may have gained much in terms of technical and artistic refinement through our specialized disciplines, but we have lost the belief that we can speak a common language or sing a common healing song.

If poetry today needs anything, it needs to move away from its insular *subjectivity*, its disdain for politics and culture and an audience beyond its own aesthetic clique. A poem reaches completion in finding an audience. The challenge today is to reach an audience not composed solely of members of one's own tribe. We must write across the boundaries of difference. A poet finds a voice by holding some sense of audience in mind during the process of composition. It is one of the questions most frequently asked of poets: for whom do you write? And the answers range from writing for posterity to writing for (or against) one's literary predecessors, from writing to an intimate other to, as Charles Wright once said, writing for the better part of oneself.

I write with an inclusive sense of audience in mind, hoping to cross the boundaries that separate people from one another. I would like to write a poem that other poets would appreciate for its formal ingenuity, that scientists would appreciate for its accuracy in attending to the phenomenal world, that the woman at the checkout counter at Safeway would appreciate for its down-to-earth soul, and that I would appreciate for its honesty in examining what troubles and moves me.

The great biology-watcher Lewis Thomas once raised the challenge:

> *I wish that poets were able to give straight answers to straight questions, but that is like asking astrophysicists*

*to make their calculations on their fingers, where we can
watch the process. What I would like to know is: how
should I feel about the earth, these days? Where has all the
old nature gone? What became of the wild, writhing, un-
approachable mass of the life of the world, and what happened to our panicky excitement about it?*

And if science today needs anything, it needs to move out of
its insular *objectivity*, its pretense that it deals only with facts,
not with ethical implications or free-market motives. What science creates is not only fact but metaphysics—it tells us what we
believe about the nature of our existence, and it fosters ever new
relationships with the unknown, thereby stirring the deepest
waters of our subjectivity. The critics of science are wrong in
saying that because of its requirements for objectivity, rigor and
analysis science has robbed us of wonder and reverence. The
methods may at times be deadening, the implications spiritually
and morally unsettling, the technology frightening, but nowhere
can one find more sources of renewal than in the marvels of the
material world, be they stellar or cellular. As Karl Popper put it,
"Materialism has transcended itself" in unveiling mystery after
mystery of process and velocity and transformation in even the
dumbest rock.

The problem is the speed at which scientific knowledge is
growing and the widening distance between those who have a
grasp of that expansion and those who have not a clue as to its
significance. During the past three hundred years, E. O. Wilson
and Charles Lumsden point out, science has undergone expo-
nential growth, meaning the larger its size, the faster it grows. In
1665 there was one scientific journal, the *Philosophical Transac-
tions of the Royal Society of London;* now there are 100,000. In the

seventeenth century there were a handful of scientists in the world; now there are 300,000 in the United States alone, and scientific knowledge doubles every ten years.

J. Robert Oppenheimer—theoretical physicist, head of the Manhattan Project that developed the first atomic bomb, opponent of the nation's postwar nuclear policy—was a man who had good cause to contemplate the ethical implications of scientific advance. In 1959 he delivered an eloquent talk titled "Tradition and Discovery" to the annual meeting of the American Council of Learned Societies, in which he spoke of

> the imbalance between what is known to us as a community, what is common knowledge, what we take for granted with each other, and in each other, what is known by man; and on the other hand, all the rest, what is known only by small special groups, by the specialized communities, people who are interested and dedicated, who are involved in the work of increasing human knowledge and human understanding but are not able to put it into the common knowledge of man, not able to make it something of which we and our neighbors can be sure that we have been through together, not able to make of it something which, rich and beautiful, is the very basis of civilized life. . . . That is why the core of our cognitive life has this sense of emptiness. It is because we learn of learning as we learn of something remote, not concerning us, going on on a distant frontier; and things that are left to our common life are untouched, unstrengthened and unilluminated by this enormous wonder about the world which is everywhere about us, which could flood us with light, yet which is only faintly, and I think rather sentimentally perceived.

Another point of contact: sentimentality is the enemy of both science and poetry.

I have in recent years been interested in the idea of the sequence, both as a poetic form and metaphorically, as the word is used to describe both the life cycle of a star and the arrangement of genes within the chromosomes. The poetic sequence, as a contemporary form, aims for a kind of fragmented connectedness in a long series of poems or a combination of poetic lines and prose; perhaps it exemplifies the idea that within chaos there is an inherent propensity for order. My book *The Monarchs: A Poem Sequence* was inspired by the migration behavior of monarch butterflies and is an extended meditation on intelligence in nature and the often troubled relationship our species has with itself and others. This excerpt will stand as my evidence that careful examination of fact yields easily to contemplation of the miraculous, that a mode of questioning we associate with science can become a nest for poetic delight.

A caterpillar spits out a sac of silk
where it lies entombed while its genes
switch on and off like lights
on a pinball machine. If every cell
contains the entire sequence
constituting what or who the creature is,
how does a certain clump of cells
know to line up side by side
and turn into wings, then shut off
while another clump blinks on
spilling pigment into the creature's
emerald green blood, waves of color
flowing into wingscales—black, orange,

white—each zone receptive only to the color
it's destined to become. And then
the wings unfold, still wet from their making,
and for a dangerous moment hold steady
while they stiffen and dry, the double-
layered wing a proto-language—one side
warning enemies, the other luring mates.
And then the pattern-making cells go dormant,
and the butterfly has mastered flight.

In ecology the term "edge effect" refers to a place where a habitat is changing—where a marsh turns into a pond or a forest turns into a field. These places tend to be rich in life forms and survival strategies. We are animals that create mental habitats, such as poetry and science, national and ethnic identity. Each of us lives in several places other than our geographic locale, several life communities, at once. Each of us feels both the abrasion and the enticement of the edges where we meet other habitats and see ourselves in counterpoint to what we have failed to see. What I am calling for is an ecology of culture in which we look for and foster our relatedness across disciplinary lines without forgetting our differences. Maybe if more of us could find ways to practice this kind of ecology we would feel a little less fragmented, a little less harried and uncertain about the efficacy of our respective trades, and a little more whole. And poets are, or at least wish they could be, as Robert Kelly has written, "the last scientists of the Whole."

Mastery for human beings is no mere matter of being the animal that we are; we will always push the limits of what we are because it is our nature to do so. The human soul is an aspect of being that comprehends no boundary, no edge. And while the world's nature will always remain evanescent to us, no matter what we do to pin it to the page, we will always find new instruments, such as electron microscopes and literature, with which to gauge the invisible.

chapter 11

The Islands

Religious man's profound nostalgia to inhabit a "divine
world" is his desire that his house shall be like the house of the
gods, as it was later represented in temples and sanctuaries.
In short, this religious nostalgia expresses the desire to live in
a pure and holy cosmos, as it was in the beginning, when it
came fresh from the Creator's hands.

—Mircea Eliade

I have a deep and abiding faith in human beings. Not necessarily in every individual human being, nor in every dip and rise of our a massing collective fortune. But considering that we are a young species, new at language, new at technology, new at learning to get along with cultural differences, new at seeing the effects upon nature of our power, we have not done such a terrible job of inhabiting the planet. And the very fact that we can imagine doing a better job is perhaps the most endearing aspect of being human, the way we ask, "What would make the world better?" "What can we do to make it so?" We go on inventing what we need to believe in ourselves. And it seems we can overcome the most horrible manifestations of human cruelty, pathological systems that make a virtue of whatever they create. We are programmed to believe in ourselves. Some of our best inventions are not things, but beautiful abstractions such as Love and God. And useful ones, such as Hannah Arendt's formulation of forgiveness, which helps us to live with being unable to undo what we have done; and promises, which are the remedy for the chaotic uncertainty of the future.

Near the time I was finishing this book, I was invited to teach for a semester at the University of Hawai'i at Mānoa. My friends and colleagues in Arizona joked, as if I were going on a permanent vacation. They cautioned that I would not like Honolulu. "It's like L.A.," they reported with disdain, "gridlock and smog and too many people." I toyed with two fantasies of the place. One, the romantic utopia of island life that frees us from urban pressures and anxieties. At least since Crusoe, islands have symbolized for Westerners the opportunity to start over from scratch with nature—one man, one little planet, and a fresh chance to get the relationship right. And the other, the dystopia of the world ruined by human beings (even isolated two thousand miles at sea!)—millions of drivers with nowhere to go, locked into their favorite machines, growling at each other like predatory beasts competing for the last prey at the end of a very long drought.

I had never visited the Hawaiian Islands, being someone who treasures solitude and avoids the tourist hot spots. The idea of a cruise fills me with socially claustrophobic dread, and most resorts suggest cruise ships to me—casting off into a compound offering a limited number of self-indulgent options available to be enjoyed with hundreds of fellow outsiders enjoying the same. And if the site of such a vacation is a place that presents itself as being made exactly for such experiences—well, count me out. I travel to see things that are strange to me, eager to know how a place has shaped its people, and how they have shaped their place. And Hawai'i, as a vacation destination, always seemed to have sold itself too well as one big resort for me to be interested in going there as a tourist. Nevertheless the enticement of a longer visit under the sanction of a job—one that would engage me with locals in thoughtful exchange—was irresistible.

I have long been interested in islands, not only because the Crusoe fantasy appeals to my own idyllic bent, but because ever since Darwin islands have been focal points for the study of evolution. Because of their geographic isolation, islands make good laboratories for examining how the process continues through adaptive radiation into separate populations that may become new species, as well as how evolution, as a process of increasing specialization and diversity, is stymied when introduced species take over habitat in rampant opportunism, crowding out vulnerable endemics. The Hawaiian Islands are upstarts in evolutionary time. Geologists say that they are a mere seventy million years old, as compared to the seven mainland continents, which are about four and a half billion years old. The Big Island is a baby, its oldest rocks above sea level "only" a million years old, and its youngest ones still pouring out and hardening. And gestating east of that is a newer island, beginning as a small underwater mountain that will appear above water in about sixty thousand years. The string of islands has been spewed out one by one as the Pacific plate drifts three inches a year toward the northwest and passes over a hot spot beneath the earth's crust through which the molten Urland seeps and boils.

If ever a place was shaped by travelers, it is Hawai'i. The islands sat lifeless in the sea for thirty-five million years. Then a few million years ago a seed drifted on wind or tide, a tree snail the size of a salt grain stuck to a bird's foot, landed and established itself on the crusty new land. Such an event took place every seventy thousand years or so. Slowly the islands began to hum with life. So isolated and pristine were the landforms that the earliest arrivals had little competition. Life was so easy that raspberries lost their thorns, stink bugs lost their stink, and the ibis and rail no longer bothered to fly. Species adapted to this place and this place alone, thriving in its biologic innocence.

Then sixteen hundred years ago, Polynesians from the Marquesas landed on the Big Island, having journeyed twenty-four hundred miles in great double-hulled canoes, guided by wayfinders skilled in navigating by the sun, stars and clouds. They brought with them what they needed to become established: pandanus for roof thatch, mats and sails; coconuts for meat, sweetening, cordage, cups and bowls; taro for making the nutritious staple poi; sugarcane, bananas, pigs, chickens and dogs.

A few hundred years later, Polynesians from the Society Islands arrived, claiming to be descended from the greatest gods and establishing themselves as rulers of Hawai'i. The culture that developed was highly stratified and guided by kapu, a complex system of traditions and prohibitions that controlled all aspects of life. The kapu system held certain people, places and things as sacred, and therefore kapu. The Hawaiians believed that their chiefs were descended from the gods: their political power came from their mana, or spiritual power. So sacred was this mana that even the chief's shadow was considered holy. To cross it was to desecrate holy ground. The chief's sanctity was protected by priests, since even a bit of hair or fingernail, or a food scrap touched by the chief, could be used in the wrong hands to steal his power. Such items were disposed of secretly by trusted attendants. A person who violated kapu might so offend the gods as to invite disaster—a volcanic eruption or tidal wave, so to sacrifice the offender was to protect the community. Punishment was the death penalty, frequently a ritual clubbing to death.

Kapu governed all aspects of life. Women ate separately from men and were not allowed to eat pork, coconuts or bananas. Fishing, planting and harvesting were strictly regulated, with natural resource managers dictating when and how foods could be taken. For all of kapu's brutality by contemporary humanitarian and democratic standards, it ensured sound conservation of resources for the centuries during which the culture evolved in relative isolation. Europeans arrived under the masthead of Captain James Cook, the British explorer, in 1778. They and their descendants, as well as multiple waves of new immigrants, caused more environmental damage in two hundred years than Polynesians had in thirteen centuries.

In the late twentieth century, the Hawaiian Islands have become a hot spot of environmental degradation caused by the alien plants and animals brought by settlers and by the rampant pace of human development. From 75 to 90 percent of all native Hawaiian bird species are gone, most of them ravaged by bird malaria introduced by mosquitoes breeding in the water barrels of the first European voyagers. Pigs and goats (the latter brought by Captain Cook as gifts to the Natives) have run wild, tearing up the forests. More than half the plants on the U.S. list of endangered and threatened species are Hawaiian. In the wet forests, introduced banana poka *(Passiflora mollissima)* vines have climbed over native vegetation, forming walls that close out the light needed by plants in the understory. In the dry forests, fountain grass (brought in by cattle ranchers) has made the habitat very flammable; 90 percent of the dry forests have disappeared, most of the damage caused by fire. Many of the native plants still hanging on have lost their insect or bird pollinators. Conservation biologists say it is too late for restoration of most of them. Where such plants remain, they can be fenced off or invasive grasses raked away once a month or so; they can be visited and monitored to see how they are doing. But they can only survive in a zoo or a garden. In certain cases of heroic dedication, they can be hand-pollinated by rappelling botanists undaunted by thousand-foot cliffs. But these plants have ceased to live freely, existing only as subjects of the human kingdom.

When I arrived on Oahu, I moved into an apartment on the edge of the forest reserve in the upper Mānoa Valley. Honolulu may be an urban sprawl, but the university neighborhood of Mānoa feels like a village. Well-tended bungalows cluster on the valley floor between symmetrical ridges that rise on two sides, rippled with fins of volcanic rock overgrown with mossy green. The ridges meet on the mauka (or mountain) side of town (as opposed to makai, the ocean side), forming a deep, lush crotch of green out of which slides a slender waterfall. Taro patches once were cultivated here, fed with the water running off the ridges. There are a few taro plants today, one or two diminutive specimens planted in a landscaped yard, or a vagrant giant with heart-shaped leaves as big as a human torso growing on the edge of the now largely cement-lined Mānoa Stream. At night the neighborhood looks like glitter spilled out on the ground, the dark heights calm and sculptural, rising into the blacker sky. The hills are high enough to catch the passing clouds, so on the mauka side of town it rains every day, fat drops pocking and ticking against the dense waxy foliage outside my screens, the wind sloshing through the trees like an omnidirectional tide, so that the trees lean and sway and swirl like jellyfish in an ocean of air.

The shape and scale of the valley is deeply appealing. Human habitation, though dense, is in modest proportion to the harboring land. I have looked and looked at its beauty, walking several miles every day on my way to and from work—along

sidewalks, through a meadow, down a trail bordering a school-
yard and through a winding back alley—trying to find the language to convey the spiritual power of the softly verdant cliffs
above. Natural beauty, as all cultures seem to have known, raises
the spiritual energy of the world. One does not need a specific
system of belief in order to experience this, for it is an inbred
biological capacity (E. O. Wilson's "biophilia")—we cannot help
but love the wonders of form and color and vitality in the lives
that surround us. When one feels the upwelling of that energy,
it is often accompanied by the desire to pass it on. Some people
take photographs, some write passionately in notebooks or send
letters to a loved one, some make drawings or paintings on stone
or paper, some give the joy back to the universe in the form of
prayer or chant, and some just hoot into the silence to hear their
voices fill with air and return to them.

My method is writing. It is where my love of nature meets
my need for human culture. After looking and looking at the
Mānoa Valley and trying to answer to it, I saw for the first time—
actually saw, did not just think about it—the land as mother,
with the two ridges of her sturdy thighs spread, a seam of wet-
ness marking the place of origin, and all of our human business on the flat land below, her progeny having spilled from that
place too.

Honolulu is really only a diminutive L.A., large enough to
offer an international and cosmopolitan culture, yet small
enough to encourage the kind of civility that develops in places
where people know they will see one another again. On most
days trade winds billow through the city carrying soggy particles
of the surrounding ocean, so that it is impossible to forget where
one is, no matter how urban a moment one may experience. At
Ala Moana Beach, ten minutes from the rain forest (and only
one minute from Honolulu's most extravagant shopping mall, at

once magnificently tacky and tony), one can swim among fishermen, surfers and families speaking Asian and Polynesian languages and pidgin permutations of the same, or one can swim in the pink water of sunset, measuring laps in the glass-faced skyscrapers of the city, or one can simply watch the jets come and go overhead while a muscular woman in a black bikini fiercely walks backward up and down the beach to tone her impeccable thighs. It is the Great American Beach where everyone is welcome to come and have a good time.

There is, of course, the matter of Waikiki, a clutch of designer hotels lording it over the beach like a monumental sculpture made of recycled computer chips and circuit boards, all electric grids and shiny curves and flashing movement. The pace and extent of the most recent Waikiki refurbishing of resort hotels, spurred by a boom in Japanese tourism, churned up old resentments among people who feel that they are losing the place as they have known and loved it, and losing their say in its future. Karl Kim, professor of urban planning at the University of Hawai'i, has compiled impressive data about the investment of Japanese companies during the late 1980s. Among the most spectacular sales: the Hawaiian Regent Hotel ($207 million), Hyatt Regency Waikiki ($245 million), Maui Marriott ($150 million), and the Big Island's Mauna Kea Resort ($315 million). The last of these was built in 1965 by Laurence Rockefeller, was the first resort on the Kohala shore, and set the local standard for luxurious grandiosity. "The strong relationship," writes Kim, "between tourism and foreign investment is evidence that Japanese firms are establishing and purchasing businesses abroad in order to capture profits from their own citizens as well as others in the international marketplace. This suggests that Hawai'i has become an economic colony of Japan."

Native Hawaiians are the most angry. They have seen foreign

investment in their homeland by business interests during the plantation era come and go, and they continue to suffer the hardships of being on the wrong side of the widening have/have not chasm. "All we get to be is the servants," said one street vendor weaving pandanus baskets and bowls for tourists, when I asked how he felt about all the tourists. In many respects, Hawai'i today is our most international state. As one visiting friend said, "This may be the United States, but it's not America anymore." And its cultural mix is no mere circumstance. Big-business plantation owners brought contract laborers to Hawai'i from wherever labor was cheapest: successive waves of Chinese, Portuguese, Japanese, Korean, Filipino, Mexican and Puerto Rican immigrants. Add to that the influx of seven million visitors every year from all over the world, and the place truly is, if not the global village, the global archipelago. Considering the ways that diverse cultures have met in the past, Waikiki is relatively self-contained and benign: a few city blocks filled with people from all over the world having a good time together out in public, watching Elvis impersonators and hula dancers, renting snorkels and surfboards, sporting happy new clothes imprinted with palm trees and hibiscus flowers, eating pad thai and burgers and mahi mahi, and having their photographs taken with a cockatoo posed on their heads. One can avoid the place if it offends or displeases of course—though not without heartache and rage, if one has known it in the homegrown stage.

Native Hawaiians once believed that spiritual guidance was available to them through 'aumākua, or guardian spirits. Many legends collected in Martha Beckwith's *Hawaiian Mythology* tell of these special relationships. These spirits might take the form of an owl, a lizard, a freshwater prawn or any other animal. A warrior in the thick of battle nearly plunged over a precipice, but an owl flew up in his face, and alerted him to danger so that he stuck his spear in the ground to stop himself from falling. A man was lost at sea when his canoe capsized. He swam all night and would have gone under had not an owl flapped its wings in his face and directed him to land. Beckwith also recounts the famous Oahu story of the owl war that was

> carried on in behalf of a man named Kapoi who, having robbed an owl's nest, took pity on the lamenting parent and returned the eggs. He then took the owl as his god and built a heiau for its worship. The ruling chief Kakuhi-hewa, considering this an act of rebellion, ordered his execution, but at the moment of carrying out the order the air was darkened by flying owls which had come to his protection.

The owls made many rendezvous for this battle, and the places where they had met were known by having the word "pueo" (owl) in their names, among them Kala-pueo east of Diamond Head and Kukaeunahio-ka-pueo (confused sound of owls rising in masses) at Waikiki.

Most popular of all family guardians was the shark ʻaumākua. Many legends, "told as actual occurrences," recount special relationships between people and individual sharks. If a corpse was offered to an animal chosen for this purpose, the family would witness the shark's skin transform to correspond with the clothing in which the beloved's body had been wrapped. This ʻaumā kua then became the family's pet. They would feed it, and it would drive food into their nets and save fishermen who were in danger.

Beckwith recounts the story of a thirteen-year-old girl living on a long sandy beach near Naalehu on the Big Island who dreamed repeatedly that a lover came to her out of the ocean. When she told her father this, he thought that "she had allowed someone liberties and wanted to conceal it, so he kept her carefully guarded." The dreams continued, and in due time the girl gave birth to a shark. Her parents recognized this offspring as a gift of the shark god and did not hold her responsible. The girl wrapped the baby in green seaweed and cast it into the sea. The shark, recognizable by its green coat, became the 'aumākua of that family and a favorite of the community. The family never again ate shark meat nor that particular seaweed, and the green shark never ate human flesh.

One day a stranger went fishing near Naalehu and was attacked by two man-eating sharks. When he cried for help, a small green shark raced to his aid, slashed the attackers with its tail until they fled, then slid under the fisherman's canoe and carried him to shore. The fisherman was so grateful that the next day he made an offering to the shark of a huge 'awa root and cleaned the barnacles and pebbles from its back. After that the man and the green shark became friends. The shark would chase schools of fish toward shore, and whatever the man caught he divided with the shark.

Many of these old legends are parables of reciprocal justice. The 'aumākua were not entirely friendly spirits and might be employed to wreak vengeance upon one's enemies. To take an example, a bird hunter slaughtered many plovers, even when he did not need them to eat. His neighbor worshiped the plover god and was sickened from the smoke of the bird hunter's oven. He warned against the sacrilege, but the bird hunter ignored him. Soon afterward a flock of plovers invaded the hunter's house, pecking and scratching him to death.

These legends, lost even to most contemporary Hawaiians, taught people to pay attention to nature for what lessons it might teach. Over the past two centuries, such beliefs in the islands have been diluted by a flooding of outside influences—European colonialism, Christian missionaries, plantation business, American pop culture and international resort development. While I have no way of knowing what the old legends mean to contemporary Hawaiians—whether they sound as made-up to them as Aesop's fables do to me, or whether the stories still retain the hum of spiritual resonance with which they once were told—I do know there are many places on the islands where one sees offerings of food wrapped in its leaves or a little tower of stones left on a beach or crater as a gift for whatever sacred power resides there.

There is, however, much dispute about who is making these offerings. Many locals say only tourists do. One wildlife tour operator said that the old Hawaiians hold each stone as sacred in its place, so to pick them up and rearrange them would be more sacrilegious than reverent. I asked a park ranger at Kilauea Volcano about the contemporary sense of ʻaumākua. She thought that people still believed in the guardian spirits, but no longer believed that they offered protection from the forces of natural disaster. For that they turn along with the rest of us to the counsel and protection of science.

Some Hawaiians are trying to recover the old ways by learning their ancestors' prayers and chants, reconnecting with sacred sites and ritual, replanting taro loʻi (the traditional method of growing the staple crop in flooded plots like rice paddies), and advocating Hawaiian sovereignty. The most inspiring story of the Hawaiian movement for cultural recovery is that of Kahoʻolawe, the smallest of the major Hawaiian islands, and one richly marked with a history of ritual and legend. For many decades it was stripped to the bone by sheep and goats. In 1941 the U.S. government claimed the island for bombing practice, and continued to shell it until as recently as the 1980s in training for Operation Desert Storm. Pualani Kanaka'ole Kanahele, a Native Hawaiian spiritual leader, credits the American Indian Freedom of Religion Act of 1978 with encouraging Hawaiians "to insist that the spiritual significance of Kaho'olawe be recognized." After many grim years of activism and court actions against the Navy (and the martyred lives of two young men attempting to occupy the island in protest), the military occupation was stopped, and in 1994 the island was rededicated as the symbolic homeland of Hawaiian sovereignty.

Even so, the process of honoring and restoring the place is not an easy one, nor can it rely solely on the old ways. Removing unexploded and poisonous ordnance on and around the island requires the expertise of military engineers. Revegetation requires the knowledge of conservation biologists. And even spiritual regeneration requires scholarly skills. In preparing to reconsecrate the site, members of the Protect Kaho'olawe Ohana researched the appropriate ancestral rituals to be performed. None of them had participated in their culture to the extent of understanding how the Makahiki—the traditional three-month celebration of the fertility god Lono—ought to be conducted. It had been 163 years since Native Hawaiians had last performed the rites. Nevertheless, Kanahele believes that the spiritual power remains, whether or not people know it. "The initial contact one has with the world of the unseen is simply a sense of 'feeling,' " she writes; and the only inkling of spiritual presence may be a vague intuition, a sudden attention shift or intensity. Learning what one is to do with such inklings is the substance of the cultural recovery continuing today in the islands, as native Hawaiians struggle to nurture a land and culture that neither U.S. statehood nor international commercial interests have served to protect.

After our weekly classes, my graduate students and I gathered at Mānoa Gardens for beer and talk about the state of the world. I have never worked with a more diverse group of individuals, each one a multicultural phenomenon. One was an East Indian businessman who grew up in Sierra Leone and runs a data-entry company serving clients on the mainland through the computer labor of workers in the Philippines. He told of having visited a village in India where youngsters attending an after-school computer class were picked up by their fathers riding on camels. We've almost solved the problem of production, he said. Soon everyone will be able to have what they want. But we haven't solved the problem of distribution, argued the Marxist African-American basketball player from Berkeley, citing who gets left out economically—the growing split between rich and poor, the lack of justice in the free-market frenzy.

I joined in—the most monochromatic of the bunch as a pale-faced New Englander—insisting we cannot speak of human progress without counting the cost other species are paying for our success. I've been reading about hominid evolution, I said, and about how we're genetically best suited to live in small kinship groups—at most one to two hundred people. We haven't yet got an ethical system to deal with the complexity we've become, so no wonder we are confused. A young Californian of Austrian heritage told of attending high school in a Catholic monastery and of his disillusion with the politics of the monastery's moral system that resulted in his getting kicked out. He took up surfing, which he practices with the intensity of a monk, and he spoke about the sacred tradition of surfing among Hawaiians, and about how proud he is to have earned the respect of locals through his courage and skill on the big waves. A woman of mixed European ancestry who grew up on Long Island, New York, but has lived for twenty-seven years on the Big Island (where she makes paintings depicting the old Hawaiian gods and legends), spoke about her understanding of the sacred as transcending religion and culture. It sounded pretty ethereal to rest of us, especially after a couple of beers. Everyone agreed that for all the gains in individual freedom and rights democracy has won, there was no longer a common ethical system for Americans, no real sense of the sacred as something absolute, unquestioned and inviolable to guide us.

Among my students were two women of Japanese ancestry, one a retired Episcopal schoolteacher and the other, much younger, a former social worker. Though they are thirty years apart in age, both were struggling in their writing to understand the impact World War II had on family members who lived in Hawai'i when Pearl Harbor was attacked. Those relatives had known themselves as Americans, but when, through none of their own doing, they suddenly became "the enemy" to both their native homeland and to their adopted country, the cultural wound was so profound that fifty years later their children and grandchildren are still trying to heal it. There was also a young man of Hawaiian, Chinese and Japanese ancestry who had worked for a time killing wild goats that were ravaging ranch and park lands on Maui, and who subsequently wrestled in his art to make peace with the necessary violence he had inflicted. And there was the Native Hawaiian still angry two hundred years later that Captain Cook and the others had showed up in the islands. It wasn't Christianity that did the natives in, he said, but the diseases the Europeans brought. I offered in appeasement that the Europeans didn't understand at that time how the diseases were transmitted. They knew what had happened in other places, he accused: when they got there, Native people died. They should have stayed home until they figured out what caused it.

There are moments in such conversations when, despite all disagreements, each person leans back from the table and looks around at the others, astonished and grateful that the world has progressed at least far enough for us to sit together and try to understand the follies and fate of our species. We know more about the world, about the beliefs and crimes of our ancestors and everyone else's, than any other people who have lived. Perhaps democracy is in its infant stage—analogous with the point in history at which Americans first began to cultivate the diminutive strains of native corn. Culture is both the crop we grow and the soil in which we grow it. It is our key survival strategy, and it has become the key survival strategy for most other forms of life on earth. This is the human power, employed by intention and accident, that we find so difficult to acknowledge.

Every trend line, from global warming to resource depletion to the extinction crisis and the bleeding out of the world of lifeways based deeply in nature, attests to what we have done wrong. E. O. Wilson, David Quammen and Bill McKibben, among others, have written the books stating the case based in science. To know that we are one with nature at this point in history is not to know a deep harmony but to know the complexity and wounding we have made, to fear and lament that it is too late to simply leave nature alone and let it take care of itself. We have made a mess of things and there is no one else but us to clean it up. We need to foster a new kind of development that is at least as committed to natural and cultural success as it is to the economic. The globalization of culture means that—full of our

cranky differences, wounded by history, and gentled by having
the long view—we have new opportunities to learn from different traditions, to see our cultural values in the context of others, to ask each tradition what it can offer to set us in a right
direction, carrying forward those aspects of culture that foster
beauty, justice, delight in life, spirituality and the integrity of nature. "Democracy," writes Václav Havel, "requires a certain kind
of citizen—one who feels responsible for more than personal
wealth—who holds ideas about democracy at the deepest
level—at the level that religion is held, where beliefs and identity are the same."

The Black Sand Beach is gone, though many "tropical paradise"
photographs still celebrate its grand and elegant arc, sheltered by
gleaming coconut palms. The village of Kalapana is gone, the
ancient temple ruins gone, the green canopy of palms gone. Past
a "Road Closed" sign, the highway lies thirty feet deep under
black, iridescent lava from the flow that began fifteen years ago
and has not stopped. I hike out over the hardened surface, past
crumbling fists of lava, and over terrain that looks like black
meringue, swirled and peaked and cracked with fissures. A trail
is barely visible where the lava has lost its shine from footwear.
The stark new earth is as solid and quiet as anywhere wild I have
walked, though this particular stretch of ground emerged from
the earth's hot mantle only seven years ago. All of this destructive creativity, it seems, ought to have a sound.

   The air is cloudy and stinks of Pele's bad weather—Pele, the
volcano goddess. Five miles down the coast a huge plume rises
where lava continues to pour into the ocean, white steam bil-
lowing and spreading into a gray pall that covers the coast for as
far as I can see. Underfoot there is not a speck of soil, only a few

cinder crumbs that have broken loose from the volcano's paving project. Sword ferns have taken root in creases, seams and cracks—anywhere a spore and some moisture might lodge. Green has never looked so electric as do these pioneers on the black lava shield.

I follow the dim trail to the ocean and find that a new black sand beach is beginning where lava has shattered into particles as it meets the sea. The beach is too small and the water too rough for anyone to be swimming or sunbathing. But three or four small rock piles have been built along the shoreline as offerings to Pele, whose whims and angers build land and swallow towns. And coconut palms have been planted wherever the sand gives their roots a purchase, the seedlings at most knee-high after six years of growth; each splitting fruit from which a stalk grows is surrounded with stones to protect it from water and wind and visitors like me. Their stiff fronds click in the breeze, and I keep startling at the sound, thinking footsteps are approaching across the crisp cindered ground.

Odd how we measure time, saying the Big Island is five hundred thousand years old when in fact it is still being born. People find meaning in answering to that process. By building and planting, they honor the form-making spirit of Earth. But there is one difference. Pele does not weep over the destruction she inflicts in her building projects. *We* are the animal that cannot accept the destruction it causes, that hears not just an inkling but a cry coming out of the world and feels spirit rise. Maybe this is the voice of our 'aumākua, a guardian spirit born of the creatures we have driven out of existence. It cries louder and louder trying to get our attention above the noise.

I walk back over the silent lava shield, past the nursery of vibrant coconut palms toward the lava-paved road. The hillside above is rich with greens, some lined up in tended rows and some exploding wild. All stages of living nurture are here side by side—the beginning, middle and end—not in sequence but simultaneous. To know myself, if only for a moment, as part of the beginning is to know the earth's sacred strength. I buy a Coke and a papaya at the Black Sand Beach Drive Inn, flip through a photo album showing the progress of Pele's neighborhood improvement project. The woman tending the counter tells me how great the beach used to be and how far she has to drive now to go swimming. "Are you sure you don't want three for a dollar," she asks, gazing ruefully at two crates of golden fruit just picked from neighborhood trees. "Well, yes, I guess I do," I say, and I choose two more at different stages of ripeness. Twenty yards behind her, the edge of the lava is frozen into a lifeless wave. She tells me to come back at sunset to see how beautiful the flowing magma is, reflected in the plume.